RACE FOR WHAT?

*A white Man's Journey & Guide to
Healing Racism from Within*

By
JD Mass, PsyD

R4W INC

St Louis MO

Copyright © 2022 Jesse Mass

All rights reserved. No part of this book may be reproduced or used in any manner without prior written permission of the copyright owner, except for the use of brief quotations in a book review.

To request permissions, contact the publisher at info@raceforwhat.com

Paperback ISBN: 979-8-9854838-0-2

Ebook ISBN: 979-8-9854838-1-9

Audiobook ISBN: 979-8-9854838-2-6

First paperback edition March 2022

Edited by: Adeyemi Franklin
Khaya Osher

Cover Designed by: Adeyemi Franklin

Cover Photo from University City High School Prom 1993

Author Headshot Photo on Back Cover by: Suzy Gorman

R4W INC
St Louis MO

https://raceforwhat.com

Table of Contents

Introduction 1

Chapter 1
Nurtured By Black Folk 11

Chapter 2
"That's how shit goes" 18

Chapter 3
Me and My Black Coaches 30

Chapter 4
Realizing the Extent of My Privilege 36

Chapter 5
Shooting to the Top with Nelly 45

Chapter 6
Meeting The African Hebrew Israelites 59

Chapter 7
What a Prestigious World We Created 73

Chapter 8
My Growth in the Kingdom of Yah 82

Chapter 9
Becoming a Father to Black Children 97

Chapter 10
    The Struggle to Fit In 112
Conclusion of My Life Stories Transitions to My Steps 125
Step 1 129
    Don't Move – Seek Understanding 129
Step 2
    Acknowledge the Harm 140
Step 3
    Letting Go of Privilege, Power and Fear 158
Step 4
    Appreciating the Value of Others 171
Step 5
    The Case for Reparations 182
Step 6
    Being Led by a New Mind 197
Step 7
    Manifesting Our Humanity 221
Thank You for Reading 236
Bibliography 243

Introduction

Some of us still need our eyes opened to the humanity of black folk. The lion's share of white people are at an epic crossroads of actually making radical, lasting change on the one hand, and utterly failing to seize this historic opportunity on the other. On the whole, we need to cut the public relations and break through to the next level of anti-racism.

Our issue is no longer apathy or ignorance. Our issue now is seeing the way forward through the fog of debate over semantics, political distractions, and self-congratulation. We need to finish the journey we started. It is time we finally repair the harm we have intentionally caused. And would it hurt to have passion for the healing that is long overdue?

This book is my vision for how we can do that...

It's a beautiful summer day in St. Louis, and my dad and I are inside OR Smoothie Cafe, passionately debating politics.

"We are in a better place now that Biden is president," my dad, Larry, a private practice attorney, argues.

My heart crunches into a ball of skepticism, my mind racing. All I can think about is how Hilary Clinton seemed so outraged at what happened in Flint, MI while campaigning during 2015-2016. As soon as she beat Bernie in the democratic race, not one peep. My next thought was how many prisons were built under Bill Clinton and how Biden was such a passionate advocate for the criminal system advancement at that time, saying some horrible things about those being targeted.

"It's so easy to say that Dad, but frankly, I'm tired of it. Biden hasn't done one damn thing for black folks in this country! He talks a sweet game and acts like he cares. Too often, we liberals become so satisfied with having 'the conversation' that we have dropped the ball on taking meaningful reparative actions. Biden's fake ass is no different than any other politician!" I say. It was a triggered response of frustration in the comfort of speaking to my father.

"You are not going to persuade anyone talking like that, Jesse!" My dad retorts.

"See, that's the problem!"

As I pause to slurp my smoothie, my mind jumps to the sole reason why I wrote this book. More than a year after the police murdered George Floyd, we whites have slipped back into the comfort zone. Many of us marched for black lives, got hip to the reality of modern racism, and elected Biden as the President who we felt would usher in a new era. But, in all of our responses to that moment, we somehow have lost our way to finishing the job we started. A job that, during the uprising even President George W. Bush said it's time to address. Not that he cares to get in front of it. If he did, he would still be demanding it. That's my concern. It is beyond time!

"Dad, I know you understand where I'm coming from," I joke, reminding him exactly of the son he raised.

Because when you look at who I am and where I've been, where I stand should come as no surprise.

***

Introduction

I am a white American Jewish man who has spent his whole life being loved by and loving black people. Both of my parents are white, and they made it their mission to raise me in a diverse neighborhood where I was exposed to the humanity of melanated folk and the dangerous flaws of racism. By the time I took the prom picture on the cover, I was 17, and all my friends were black. With brothers like these, I truly lived Dr. King's dream. I was blessed with a mesmerizing childhood filled with boisterous family gatherings at Ma's house, playing every sport imaginable, and talking smack all day.

Not long after we took this picture, I became an emboldened adult who eventually ditched a banking career to become Nelly's business manager. From helping Nelly break into the NASCAR industry to helping pioneer Apple Bottoms, an urban clothing line for curvy women, I was that white man in the room we often felt we needed to broker multi-million dollar deals. Desiring to make my life's work with black folk, I later traveled to Israel, joined forces with the African Hebrew Israelites, and helped expand their pioneering soul vegan imprint in Los Angeles (LA). My journey also led me onto the path of fathering black children, becoming an activist, and earning a PsyD in Organizational Psychology with a goal to transform organizations into diverse workplaces filled with humanity *and* productivity.

Throughout my journey, I have witnessed the depth of racism and struggled with my own white savior syndrome. I have delved deep within my introspection to find answers and gained the wisdom to better understand how much black human beings want to lead themselves.

I am here to offer my fellow white folks a vision of a pathway out of the abyss of the anti-racism fight and into the final steps necessary to complete the mission. While I know that there are other groups and other issues that are not just black and white (melanated and low-melanated), I'm writing this book from my personal perspective and experiences. It is not my intention to offend anyone or speak on what I am not familiar with. While you may disagree with my views, I'm asking that you take the time to read my story, try to understand where I am coming from and how what I am suggesting may be of some benefit for individuals and society as a whole. In the future, I am interested in learning more about other groups and issues and seeing how I can be an instrument of change for the better.

A few caveats before reading further:

Have you ever noticed how those who are part of a group of "privilege" become uncomfortable, sometimes even defensive, when some of those who are not part of the "privileged" group start talking about their circumstances? For example, a group of men might get uncomfortable around some women who start discussing some aspect of feminism even if those comments are not directed at those men in particular.

White folks have a tendency to feel quite uncomfortable when race is a topic of discussion. You may find that some of what I say in this book creates a level of discomfort. While my intention is to provide food for thought, you may even get offended. All I ask is that you read with an open mind and take a moment and ask yourself, "Why am I reacting to this? Is there any validity here to what is being said? How does my level of discomfort compare to what melanated humans experience?" These are questions that I have asked myself throughout my journey.

As I talk about the issues of white culture, I am in no way suggesting that any or all the problems that need to be addressed are solely unique to white folks. For example, slavery existed before colonialism. It was not nearly as violent and atrocious as we created it. Nonetheless, it did exist as a kind of indentured servitude, often to work off a debt. Many groups of all shades and geographical areas have desired to dominate others, used deceitful tactics, and caused harm to other humans and the planet. The fact that other cultures have caused harm to other groups of humans and the environment does not take away from what I am addressing in our white Greco-Roman culture that has attempted to colonize the planet.

In many ways, no culture has been as violent, brought forth as much disease, and caused as much harm to the planet. I believe that this has to do much more with how we feel about ourselves. I am attempting to uncover how we react and emote our feelings about our low-melanated skin and the effects on the areas of the planet we occupy. I want us to address our behaviors and partake in the healing process. We can learn to be great contributors in an honest and open society. Race has nothing to do with our capabilities to do so.

As you read about the Hebrew Israelite community later in my journey, it is essential to know they have faced many challenges as they have tried to progress, many of which have been driven by racism. While they were focused on developing their culture, they were seen as a threat to Israelis by the Israeli leadership. Many attempts using physical intimidation, chemical warfare, and economic deprivation have caused harm and remain obstacles to reaching their desired vision.

Internally the community struggles with the elder regime not letting go of control and causing dissension among them and the younger generations. Many have left, and many are still being introduced and joining them. Yet, they are 50 years old. While they have areas in which they can improve, they have also had many successful demonstrations of improving many lives in various countries worldwide. I am sharing some of what I experienced in this book. The vision and teachings are what are important to me moving forward. There are many new ideas on how to live and build a humane community and bring forth positive outcomes in the world. This community is the one I experienced that had the greatest impact on me.

In this book, you will see that I use aboriginal and or indigenous when describing black and other melanated humans. I understand that we have often associated aboriginal as meaning the black folk of Australia. However, the term is rooted in original, and Africa is where the original human beings are from. Having darker skin is an original skin color, whereas lighter skin tones are not. I use these terms to describe people of color because they give a different feeling than using black, brown, yellow, or white. It makes us think differently about how we see humans with different skin tones than ourselves. We lack something that existed in the original form, and we must deal with what that means for us as we look to heal the harm we have caused.

In writing this book, using what some would consider more "proper" or "sophisticated" language has not been my focus for three reasons. First, English has never been my strongest subject, even though I achieved higher levels of education. Second, my focus was on the book's message and having it come as much as possible from my voice. Third, I want my message to be accessible for everyone, not impress those with greater vernacular abilities.

Together we will dive into seven steps, have even tougher conversations, and finally move forward in the right direction.

Introduction

These seven steps will require us to ask different questions and ultimately overcome persistent psychological blocks, allowing us to:

- Ask ourselves why we created race in the first place
- Acknowledge the harm we've done to the planet and humanity
- Learn to let go and allow ourselves to be open to new possibilities
- Learn to appreciate the contributions of black folk
- Repair the harm through reparations
- Go forth with a new mind
- Manifest a humane way of life

Along the way, I will take you on my life journey to this point. For as powerful as black love has been to me, it didn't save me from the arrogance of my whiteness, nor did it save me from myself.

In 2017, I found myself living out of my car after more than a decade of struggling to maintain in LA. Sitting in the driver's seat without any big jobs to go to, the past fourteen years of my life played out in my mind with painstaking hindsight and regret. In 2004, I had abruptly quit working with Nelly after months of misunderstandings. Just a year prior, I was one of the leaders positioning Nelly for unprecedented business success. I had helped Nelly start several other ventures, poised to make many millions of dollars. Riding high, I even married the President of Apple Bottoms. Throughout, a staunch white savior syndrome blinded me from understanding the cultural differences of Nelly and his organization, leading me to make numerous mistakes. When I walked away, it was indeed the biggest defeat in my life. Not long after, my marriage spiraled toward divorce.

Instead of seeking work elsewhere, I strove to make a name for myself as an entrepreneur in the industry. With a few new clients on my plate, I thought I had what it took to be a part of their successful careers, but they all fell through. I didn't have the relationships to start with unknown artists, and I didn't bring the value of the Nelly name to the industry execs with whom I had built ties.

Soon after letting go of that dream, a fateful life twist reintroduced me to the African Hebrew Israelites, and I began turning my life around. I joined forces with their community in LA to make it big in their vegan soul food enterprise. Again, my arrogance – combined with ignorance – led to fighting and eventually losing funds and friendships. My lowest point was in 2010 when my final chance to structure a new venture to keep our dream afloat fell apart.

From all this loss and pain, I had to make sense of my life. I knew I was called to build powerful alliances with black people. Still, on a deeper level, I had to confront my whiteness and accept the role of racism in the broader society that made each leap we took nearly an impossible riddle. In the end, I had to grapple with the unfinished business in my life and our world. I began to focus and open my mind to the possibility of genuinely completing the healing that needed to take place.

This profound self and societal examination have culminated in this book, which comes at a heightened time in this exhausting fight to end racism.

Many of you politically are at the same point I was in my personal life: fired up about black lives but at a loss about how to maintain bonds and get past personal ego to a new way of being. Many of you, as I did with Nelly and the Hebrew Israelites, have given your all and are still not getting the results you need to see to keep going.

Trust me - I know what it feels like to be stuck and stagnant on the journey to realizing the dream. I am here to tell you that we can stay the course and finish the work we started! White people, we can end racism!

In this book, I share my life as inspiration and my lessons as navigation to drive our new consciousness to the final destination.

Born of my many successes and failures as a white man, and out of my struggle to build alongside black folk, to father black children, and to be a force of change without arrogance - this book will help us break out to the next level of evolution. If my journey to this point is of no consequence to you and you are more interested in my vision for healing, I encourage you to skip my narrative and go to the steps I have suggested.

Race for What?

'Race for What?' is a turning point. It's a question and a commentary. Why did we whites create racism in the first place is what we must ask ourselves before we go any further. How does race continue to plague our progress as humans, and how can we unpack the psychological factors that continue to fuel racism?

While we whites are constantly racing to dominate the world, the deeper question is what for?

After examining these questions and more, we will get to the very heart of ending racism.

Though the way forward is perplexing, we will complete this epic journey and bring forth a better world for others and the planet.

1

Nurtured By Black Folk

Loving yet stern, Maxine opened my eyes to the inner magic of the black world. For in that world, I found a deep kind of nurturing that continues to inspire me today. One of my fondest childhood memories is of me going to Maxine's home daycare in Philly. I'll never forget how she'd squat down to my level, look me in the eye, and speak lovingly but firmly, telling me how to play and share with others.

Since I was a shy kid, she'd also make a fuss, saying, "You've got to tell me what's going on, or I can't help you." Every day, I looked forward to her diligent care, her home-cooked meals, and trips to the park with the other kids who she loved equally. Shortly before my sister Jenny (who later changed her name to Khaya) was born, Maxine drew me close and explained how important it was to be a big brother. "Make sure she always feels loved," she'd say, her auburn curls resting on her pretty brown face. Not long after that talk, my family moved to St. Louis, Missouri. By then, however, Maxine had left an indelible impression on me.

In the Lou, my family set down roots in University City, a suburb known in St. Louis as U. City. U. City was a vibrant and diverse community. Diversity in St. Louis was hard to come by so in that way

U. City was unique. Next door to our new home lived the Jordans, a big, boisterous family that would impact my life forever. Ruled by a remarkable matriarch everyone called "Ma," the Jordans made up nine children and grandchildren who grew to be like family to me. I became best friends with Ma's oldest grandsons, Mike and Shando, and together, we came of age in the streets and playgrounds of St. Louis.

With Mike and Shando, no sport or joke was off-limits. We played kickball, wiffleball, and ran bases. Best of all, we played a tackle football game we called Killaman. Mike and Shando were always much taller than me, but in Killaman, I began to earn their respect by using my heart to will me through their tackles or try to take them down at the knees. We were rough kids, to say the least, ending everything we did with a game of hitting each other with objects, be it acorns, small sticks, or rocks. With every howl of "Ouch!" we laughed harder, which in turn, brought us closer and closer together.

When not roughing around, Mike, Shando, and I dove into making extra bucks by raking leaves, landscaping, cleaning up, or shoveling snow. We'd then run straight to the corner store to buy Chocolate Paydays and Now and Laters. One time, we put together a backyard play and charged our family and neighbors $1 a ticket. Afterward, Shando and I performed in concert, rapping "My Adidas" by Run DMC and "My Radio" by LL Cool J. I distinctly recall my grandparents staring at me with their jaws dropping in disbelief as their once little shy grandson rapped with the confidence of New York's finest hip-hoppers.

Like my biological family, the Jordans gave me tough love. "Messy Jesse" is what they called me, teasing me until I developed tough skin. One time, when I was about eight years old, I yelled out,

"Damn," soon realizing Ma was in earshot range. My heart raced, anticipating her reaction. But Ma very gently said, "Jesse, I don't know what you can get away with at your house, but if I ever hear you say something like that again, I will handle it my way." All I could say was, "Yes, Ma'am." Scared but relieved, I decided I would never curse at Ma's house again.

The more time I spent with the Jordans, I also learned invaluable lessons about siblinghood. Despite Ma's grandchildren's fights, they would always come back together and stand up for one another. Mike and Shando and their brothers Lee and Robert learned to encourage and support one another no matter what. In turn, once my little sister Khaya started to sprout, I took pride in being her older brother. I knew she looked up to me, and as time went on, her mix of friends increasingly looked like mine: black.

When I was seven and a half, my youngest sister Paula was born. At birth, doctors diagnosed her with down syndrome, a genetic disorder that causes developmental delays. Despite her condition, Paula developed a sparkling personality. She was a tease and as sarcastic as any of us in the family. She loved movies and television shows and would watch and share her thoughts about characters or use lines from movies whenever they fit into a conversation. She wasn't afraid to insert herself socially into conversations, so my friends grew to love her quite easily.

I learned from Ma's family and my parents to always be proud of her. In fact, Darnita, Shando and Mike's mother, became Paula's best friend for several years as her caretaker after Khaya and I had left the house. Paula pushed us to appreciate who people are and their differences. Eventually, Paula became a superstar in our school district, and I was proudly known as Paula's brother.

Day by day, the Jordans drew me out of my shell and taught me invaluable life lessons. They nurtured my existence as if I was one of their own. Year in and year out, the Jordans afforded me an adventure-filled and happy childhood that I can only describe as truly remarkable. To this day, I wish every child had my childhood experience.

My parents were my role models

My parents inspired me early on to value my relationships with aboriginal humans. They chose for us to live in U. City for their children and themselves, as well. They were examples in the way they treated my friends and our housekeepers and their families and anyone we interacted with in any setting. They were consistent in showing respect, especially when the humans we met were in conditions of hardship. I can remember my father taking me to volunteer at a homeless shelter. I was under ten years old and still primarily innocent to the trials and tribulations of the adult world.

Larry treated everyone he met with the same level of curiosity and enthusiasm as he would when he would meet people at his work or the tennis court. He encouraged me to introduce myself and play with the children my age during our volunteer sessions. When they invited us to eat with them at their table, we happily joined. I knew that there was a reason he wanted me to experience these moments. On the way home, we talked about what I felt and how they were no less human than us and deserved respect. Their conditions did not define their character.

Growing up with housekeepers sometimes felt uncomfortable because my friends' families didn't have that luxury. At the same time, I grew to love and appreciate my relationships with Lucille, Eunice, and especially Francis, with whom I became very close. She let me drive as soon as I was able, partially because I was a better driver than her. Seriously, she scared Shando and me when she would come to a stop in a busy street when she wanted to switch lanes.

Francis and I would go grocery shopping just for us and come home and make Rueben sandwiches. I never saw them as less than or employees. They were like family, and my parents treated them as such. They certainly cared for us that way, too. They shared in conversations with my parents about how my sisters and I would be disciplined, what to do to encourage us, and what our interests were. My mom used to tell me about how much Augusta meant to her as a caretaker. Like in the movie The Help, my mom and her mom often had an uncomfortable relationship, and she gained so much from having Augusta be there to raise her.

Whenever there was a reason for the family to get together, whether it was a holiday or to celebrate an accomplishment (can you believe JD graduated high school?!), we spent that time with the Jordan family, Augusta and her family, and the family of those who cared for my sisters and me, among other family, friends, and neighbors. It was done without effort or second thought so that it seemed natural. To my parents, it was natural. As a child, I knew it was different than what most children experience because of segregation, but I didn't think too much about it. It was just the way it should be to me, and I enjoyed it as much as I could.

I also really appreciated my parents for their efforts to include my friends. When we took trips to the movies, a ball game, or a weekend or summer trip out of town, I could invite a friend or two. When we went shopping for clothes, my friends were not only invited but also allowed to pick out items they wanted too. It was never done as charity. It was always out of love. My parents were interested in my friends' well-being and wanted to give them a chance. My father was their lawyer. He was also their father figure, and they knew to act right when he was around. My mother was the community doctor for physicals to play sports or to write a prescription when they were in need. Both of my parents invested in my friends' growth and development.

When it was time to hang out, the fridge and food on the shelves were available to anyone who visited. Whether it was me and my friends or my sisters and theirs, our kitchen was a shared kitchen. No one was being served after the first visit. You get your own food and beverages. The feeling was no different than when my friends and I hung out at the Jordan family or over at Nelly's house. Ms. Mack, Nelly's mama, became Mama to all of us. Shando's grandma was always going to be Ma to all of us. The fact that my parents were the same – welcoming and willing to help just with different opportunities and financial capabilities – made it simple to see that we all share in common the way we see family and community.

Awakened by Dr. King's dream

One day, my outlook on life suddenly had direction. I was in the 3rd grade and finally learned about Dr. King. Though his life resonated with what my progressive parents had taught me, I could not understand why Dr. King had become famous for what seemed like an evident belief - that all people are equal. I remember sitting at my desk mortified that a man had to give his life to convince people that we are all worthy of love, fairness, and justice. When I pressed my teacher for answers, I realized nothing she said would diffuse the seeds of discontent in my soul. Because of this, I took it as a personal charge to continue King's vision and help heal the world of racism. Although I was only eight years old, I actively began seeking out instances of racism in hopes that I could transform it somehow.

2

"That's how shit goes"

In my righteousness, I grew intolerant and rude toward anyone I detected was discriminating against black folk. In most cases, this attitude found me smarting off at my middle school teachers. If I witnessed even the slightest injustice, I would ring the alarm, saying, "You don't know what you're talking about... nuh-uh, that's not true!" I wasn't always effective. I was just comfortable being emotional about speaking up.

By the time I got to U. City High School, my defense of my black friends got even bolder. I clearly remember during my senior year when I was summoned to the principal's office after helping my friend Fat E fight off a bunch of other students. Wide-eyed, I said: "BULLSHIT! *I'm* getting suspended for joining the fight? My friend got jumped twice! The staff broke it up but did not make sure my friend was safe!"

The principal, Mr. Thatcher, a short white man with a big bald spot (sounds identical to me today), gasped then paused for what seemed like hours. I knew I had crossed the line. Thankfully, it had escalated to the point that my lawyer father had to get involved who was sitting next to me at the time. He initially scolded me, saying I did not need to use that language. Dad then turned to the principal and told him that I couldn't be more correct. Despite our protest, however, Fat E got suspended for a full ten days while I walked away with in-school suspension for a week. The look on Fat E's face is still fresh in my mind. Sunken and defeated, he thanked me for trying to help and said in surrender, "That's how shit goes."

At this point, I knew all too well the shit Fat E was talking about.

Shando and Gamal gave me "the talk"

At the age of 12, I had my first encounter with racist police. It was a Friday night, and Shando, Gamal, and I were walking home from the Galleria Mall in the suburb of Clayton. Out of nowhere, two white cops jumped out of their car, interrogating us from the jump.

"Where are you going? What are you doing out this late? Why are you walking here?"

As if these questions weren't bad enough, they said: "We are investigating a burglary not too far from here. What can you tell us about what happened?" We knew nothing about a burglary. The cops pressed on, "What is your address? We may hold you until we find more information about who committed the burglary... unless you want to tell us what happened. Are you hiding anything?" The unjust prodding continued, igniting my defenses.

Naively, I said, "We don't know anything about a burglary, but we can try to help you find what happened." Gamal snapped back, "No, we can't!" *Dang it!* I knew that I had fucked up.

The mischievous grin on the officer's face said it all. "If you don't know anything, then how can you help us? You must know something or have been involved. Why don't you tell us what happened?" I reverted back to denying knowing anything. My spirit was trembling. I worried about getting my black friends in trouble.

Fifteen excruciating minutes ticked by. Then finally, the cops let us go after threatening to give us a citation for violating curfew. On the way home, Shando and Gamal gave me "the talk." You know that conversation all black families have with their sons and daughters about how to survive racist police encounters. They hassled me for trying to play hero, telling me what to say and what not to say. "The cops aren't our friends," Shando said. "If they were, they wouldn't be bothering us."

Seeing race as a child

From the start, my family possessed a genuine love for justice. Our dinner conversations swirled with hot topics and serious issues. My father would bring up a news story then probe it from a systematic and racial justice point of view. "Jesse, the system creates an environment of despair by removing the amenities needed to live with comfort," my dad would lecture. "It then blames people for acting out of their frustrations. Many crimes we punish people for are only acts of people who feel a level of desperation."

My mom, a doctor who was always quick to chime in, talked passionately against the capitalistic decision-making structure that made proper healthcare impossible. "We as doctors are being forced to make decisions between our profits and providing diagnostic tests that can lead to real care." she would say, gritting her teeth with disgust. Because of our talks, I was uniquely primed to detect problems with colonial behavior at an early age.

One time at my Great Aunt's house, my older cousin's friends and I were watching March Madness college basketball on TV. All guys in the room, one of the guests said, "Damn, I wonder how these black guys are so good at basketball?" "It's amazing to me," another one said, "it's because they used to chase lions and tigers in Africa." They all laughed. I didn't know how to take that comment. Although they were joking, I felt like they were degrading black athletes to the level of animals. I had to leave the room. Was it jealousy? Was it malice? Considering my closeness to my black friends, I didn't find it funny at all. However, I wanted to understand why we whites held these views and began having conversations with whoever was willing to engage.

I also sought to listen to black adults and consider their points of view. At Ma's house, I listened attentively as people talked about their experiences with white folks. They spoke with frustration about being followed around a grocery store or being passed up for raises and promotions despite outperforming their white counterparts, who'd then get the promotion. Sometimes, they would vent about being talked down to by whites and not treated with respect.

By contrast, I watched white folks not act on subtle racism but rather figure out ways to justify it in their mind. For example, my dad's father, Grandpa Bob, on the one hand, would explain how he wasn't racist because he defended black construction workers as a lawyer, helping them achieve equal pay for their work. On the other hand, he would tell me how black folks were not good at managing their money, which was why they made poor business owners.

Most white people didn't see racism up-close and relied mainly on what they had heard or read in the news or societal norms that we are taught subliminally. While my parents astutely taught me about the differences in prison sentencing and how police targeted blacks at a much higher rate than whites, the news would show a scowling black face of someone who was caught committing a crime.

There was so much talk in the local news about the amount of drug use in black areas. Yet the all-white Clayton High School (other than the "deseg" students who were bussed in) was a drug dealer's dream location because these were rich kids that did heavy drugs. This phenomenon was not covered in the news, nor were those whites arrested at nearly the same rate. But we knew the Clayton kids did more drugs than any other school district. Clayton is one of the wealthier municipalities of St. Louis County.

Seeing segregation

Even with all of U. City's diversity, I started to see its segregation, which in and of itself is not a terrible thing. Kids would sit in the cafeteria according to race, and head home in opposite directions, based on race. After talking with a few friends, I learned that this type of segregation didn't strike many students as harmful. But in the context of the wider society, segregation proved to be a dangerous scheme in criminalizing black lives.

Riding along Delmar Blvd., you'd see it: the divide between blacks who lived in large, multi-family homes or smaller, single-family homes just north of the road and the white business class that inhabited lavish mansions just south of Delmar. On the black side, cop cars stayed pulling people over, whereas just yards across Delmar, cops would sit studiously in front of mansions, protecting the property from robbers. On the black side, mom-and-pop shops were shutting down as Family Dollar and Walgreens sprung up, while blocks away on the white side, upscale businesses managed to survive amidst thriving investment.

As close as they were to each other, there was potential for these two worlds to cross. But they never did. Instead, black communities were forced to live without the public financing for infrastructure, education, legal entrepreneurship, and being able to control their opportunities. These advantages came with the air we breathe in white communities without being told the truth about how much less was shared in the black communities. Instead, we whites learned how much violence took place in 'the hood,' how many black people are criminals, how many choose to be on welfare or drugs. And if a few could survive and succeed based on our definition, then we assumed that opportunity existed for all participants and that the problem was how black people thought or behaved. This cycle of racialized deprivation and investment created a level of fear about intermingling and the justification for why we need to remain separated.

One of the most surprising things I learned is how most black people responded to racism. Rather than succumbing to hate or revenge, black folk kept faith in their fundamental right to be left free, to have an equitable share, create their own comfortable lifestyle, and be recognized for the value of their culture and work. Using the little power I had, I felt my mission was to find ways to speak up when my black friends were mistreated. My father would take me to synagogue and the lawyers guild conferences where I could share with like-minded whites hoping to provide whatever inspiration I could from sharing my stories.

Preparing for my Bar Mitzvah

Around the time the police stopped us in Clayton, my family and I eagerly planned for my Bar Mitzvah, my Jewish rites of passage ceremony into manhood. I still had many questions about the world, and I found solace at Central Reform Congregation (CRC), a Jewish spiritual center led by Rabbi Susan Talve. In my father's effort to share his faith, he took me to CRC, the only synagogue in the inner city – and a mere stone's throw from 'the hood' sitting right across Delmar Blvd. Tall, kind, with flowing brown hair and purpose-filled eyes, Rabbi Talve made a name for herself in her quest for racial justice. She added a refreshing twist to the cause by redefining Jewish traditions to create a more inclusive and thriving St. Louis.

One of those traditions was hachnasat orchim or extending hospitality to strangers. Rabbi Talve did this with such a great sense of appreciation; she would acknowledge all guests and encourage me to bring my black friends. Her love of people consumed her entire life and, thankfully, trickled down to my soon-to-be 13-year-old self. Rabbi Talve welcomed me so graciously that I began inquiring how my friends could join me for Saturday School and Shabbat Services afterward. Whenever I raised a question about God, racism, or life, she was incredibly open and showed me how the teachings applied to my life.

Leading up to my Bar Mitzvah we met at her house, a block from my mom's parents, to review the process and my translation of the Torah passages I was supposed to read in Hebrew. During this time, Rabbi Talve and her husband, Rabbi Jim Goodman, became real inspirations for me. With Rabbi Talve busy fighting for racial justice and Rabbi Goodman sharing his passion for string instruments, they were two of the coolest white people I had ever met. Their home quickly became one of the few white homes I felt comfortable in.

Growing up, I was about as -ish as one could be when it came to being a Jew. I did not believe the stories of Adam and Eve being the first humans or Moses splitting the sea for only his people to pass through, as they were taught to me. The stories seemed no different from fables – good lessons to be learned from creative stories of a make-believe world. I certainly didn't believe in the relationship between humans and God as it was taught to me by Jews from the Torah or Christians from the New Testament.

My mother and I shared a certain disdain for these translations, especially the one that looks upon all white Jews as "the Chosen People." My skin would crawl every time I heard that spoken by other Jews. It seemed to spawn from a pompous attitude and arrogance that turned me off. Did they deserve something special for being chosen? I felt this view also allowed for too much wrong to be done under the guise of religious righteousness.

In an effort to rebel against these conventional notions, my mom and I would crack jokes in the pew and laugh about how arrogant some Jews can be. "They think they are so smart, but look how destructive this behavior is," I'd say. "They make me want to throw up," my mom would retort. My mom and grandma Mimi stayed by my side, making me feel comfortable. Together, they instilled in me that true spirituality was expressed by giving and helping others and that God is universal. "You are a spiritual human, not religious," Mimi would tell me. She often praised me for my willingness to help others, include and value other people, and refrain from judging people without learning about their journey.

Having black friends became a concern

As my Bar Mitzvah neared, I struggled to learn Hebrew. I didn't see how I'd use it beyond the synagogue and holidays, so I lacked interest in it. Seeing my resistance, Grandpa Bob, my dad's father, offered to give me $1000 for completing the Bar-Mitzvah successfully. Imagining the cash in hand, I suddenly felt motivated. Let the learning begin!

Being from a conservative Jewish family in a reform synagogue, I oddly enough participated in much more of the service than the usual reform Jewish bar mitzvah did. Along the way, I invited Shando to participate in my rites of passage. That seemed really cool to me until one Friday Shabbat dinner when my parents left the room. Suddenly, Grandpa Bob started to ask me strange questions about the Bar Mitzvah. As he leaned in with a look of concern for me, dropping his voice, Grandpa asked, "Are any of your black friends invited to the bar-mitzvah?" It hurt me that my friend's race was of concern. In turn, I wanted him to feel the pain of telling him the honest answer.

"Yes," I responded confidently. "Shando is going to take the Torah from the arc and hand it to me to read from it." Grandpa Bob reeled back his head, startled and appalled. "That is the most sacred part of the ceremony! How could you choose him for that role?" None of the religious traditions mattered to me, so I told him that Shando didn't read Hebrew, and I wanted him to be a part of it because he is my best friend. Grandpa Bob stood up from our table and walked into the living room where Bubby and my father were talking. "Get your things, Rose. We are leaving."

As he parted, I felt relieved and couldn't wait to tell my dad about his pops. "What happened," my father pleaded in a state of confusion. "Why did they leave like that?" I told him the truth. All along, my father had protected me from my grandpa's prejudice and felt furious that his dad would ask me those questions without my dad being there. From that day on, I began tuning into how my family addressed race. The level of prejudice surprised me. At the same time, I was beginning to realize how my dad had been defending his choice of how to raise me to his parents.

On my mom's side, Papa and Mimi seemed very inviting and welcoming to have my friends join me when they took me out. They loved Shando's jokes, especially Mimi. But it was Papa that first said a comment when Shando and I were playing in their house. Shando left a door open to the library, one of the few rooms with air conditioning. "They," (as in black people) Papa said, "don't know how to pay attention." I was nine or ten years old and remember being shocked that Papa associated this mistake with Shando's race. It wasn't until many years later did my mother bring up her father's racist views that I knew she knew.

Papa grew sick around the time of my bar mitzvah and passed away early in my high school years. That was the only time I experienced any racist response from him. Grandpa Bob was different. We had an ongoing dialogue about race following that introduction surrounding my bar mitzvah. Looking back, I appreciate our relationship more now than when I was going through it. We discussed why I lacked diversity in my friends, especially when bringing them to visit my grandparents. I explained that I did not choose my friends based on their color. From what I experienced, black students were more welcoming to the white population in the school. Still, the cultural differences may have made it somewhat uncomfortable for most of the other white students to fully immerse in black culture as I had.

That said, our white population at our school was around ten percent in middle school and even less in high school. Even though U. City had a white population of about 50% of the overall, we made up about 15% of the student base and about half that of the high school student base. Most white families sent their children to private and religious schools. I explained to Grandpa Bob that even when I did invite white friends, they did not want to come with me to his house. This included a cousin related to him. I also wasn't invited by my white friends to much of what they were doing. I was okay with that because I liked my friends, and there was no malice between the other white students and me.

Grandpa Bob wanted me to see a more diverse group of people to have greater experiences from which to learn. He tried to tell me if all of my friends were white or, more specifically Jewish, he would have told me to make friends who were black and or Christian. He then said the classic, 'I have black friends' line. The truth is, though, I never met any of them. He also told me that, as an attorney, he represented black construction workers in St. Louis to help them achieve equal pay compared to their white counterparts. I grew to learn that Grandpa Bob's concerns were a bit layered. For one, he was much more pro-Jewish than anti-black. He did not ever come across as wishing ill will towards the black community or my friends. He mainly wanted me to be more involved in the Jewish community and appreciate Jewish culture.

However, I didn't excuse Grandpa for this prejudice. At the same time, he did teach me that there is diversity among racist viewpoints. For many whites, racism comes from wanting more for themselves and their families. A zero-sum mentality in which one person's gain is seen as another's loss makes whites want to "keep it in the family." For others, racism comes from ignorance, hate, and fear of the unknown. However, both forms of racism are dangerous and destructive.

The more I tried to get answers about my family's racist viewpoints, the more I saw how people were unwilling to dig deep enough. Stats were thrown around about poverty, crime, and incarceration to justify their views of black people. And, when it came to self-policing their racism, the focus rested on racist actions and words, and not more insidious forms of racism that we whites subconsciously prop up.

In the back of my mind, I'd always wonder: what are the thoughts behind the emotions that led to this? When I see racist behaviors, systemic designs to keep people suppressed, or even the denial or purposeful ignorance related to addressing racism, the behavior seems to come from an emotional place, which stems from the thoughts we tell ourselves. A lot of it seemed like jealousy and a projection of our ideas of self onto others.

What I mean is that we portray blacks as violent and fear them wanting revenge, but the truth is, if we realize these are our emotions and look for personal experience of such portrayals, they do not exist enough to warrant those prejudices. If we are going to fully address the transformation at the level of healing that is needed, then these improvements will come from addressing the emotional state of racism and psychology and intentional behaviors that result from these emotions.

I continued on my path

As my friends and I grew older and were able to drive, they would go every day or night to a different basketball gym in another area of St. Louis. I joined as much as I could. Through my relationship with Shando, I was introduced to and strengthened my relationships with those who became our high school crew. For me, this was also a chance to get to experience and observe life within different black communities.

There was always a crowd, and I was often the only low-melanated human there. There were many occasions where my friends or I had to convince people that I was not the police or an informant. Sometimes a popular member of a community would approach me, and he would either test me by talking trash or be inviting. Still, I felt comfortable as the more I stayed true to who I was, the easier it was to be accepted.

3

Me and My Black Coaches

At every stage of my childhood, sports continued to be a source of camaraderie for me. It was here that black men powerfully nurtured me.

My first coach, Mr. Stevenson, profoundly affected my psyche and life development. He was a middle-aged man who I'd come to love and dearly admire. Even to this day, Mr. Stevenson's influence has been instrumental. Standing at 6'4 with a stocky build and donning glasses, he was the coach of my little league baseball team. "You couldn't catch a cold butt-naked in the middle of Alaska," he'd yell. His mix of trash talk and love inspired all of us to put forth our best effort and never give up. Where I felt like my height would be a disadvantage, Mr. Stevenson eased those fears by never expecting anything less than the best from me on the field. "You don't lose in life unless you quit," he'd say. "Only then is the game over. Otherwise, you keep learning until you accomplish your goals."

In addition to being a coach, Mr. Stevenson was the president of the Old El Paso food division of Pet Inc. He had risen through the ranks and afforded himself a nice, middle-class life. I appreciate the most how he disciplined me, allowing me to see the consequences of my decisions and anger. During a league game against our rivals, I was upset we were down big early on. "We're going to lose this game!" I said in disgust on the bench. Shando, Mr. Stevenson's son Quinn, and I had been benched to start the game for cracking jokes and being silly. Mr. Stevenson gave me the most searing look of disapproval. He put Shando and Quinn back in the game and extended my punishment an extra inning before I could return.

Despite us eventually coming back and winning the game, Mr. Stevenson used this as an opportunity to teach us all a lesson. To begin the next practice, Mr. Stevenson whipped out a notecard and read inspirational quote after quote. One of them stuck with me: "Some people see the golf shot as possible, but difficult. Other people see the golf shot as difficult, but possible," he said. That quote indeed would alter my negative attitude, helping me face the hurdles of life with more courage.

My father and Mr. Stevenson were two consistent male figures in my life and my friends' lives. Both men of tremendous achievement, they transcended race and formed a remarkable friendship. They were role models and providers not only for their families but for all of us in the neighborhood.

Thanks to their example, I began to equate manhood with the ability to take care of more than just yourself. Manhood was the graciousness to help and empower others. My father and Mr. Stevenson invested in all of us, whether it was feeding us delicious burgers after the game or driving us to decked-out facilities beyond what the local leagues provided. As a result, every step I took in life that I was proud of, I wanted to share with dad and Mr. Stevenson.

Tennis was my best sport

Shando and I learned tennis in our early childhood. At the age of 13, I left playing baseball and began to focus on playing tennis. My private coach was Mike Jones, another black man who made a big difference in my life. A former Major League Baseball Player, Mike - as we called him - stood 6'2 and had an intimidating scowl. He met me, Shando, and Gamal during our summer tennis program taught by him and another black man named Carl Walker.

Mike took a liking to me because I worked hard and followed his guidance. He asked my parents to allow him to coach me three days a week for two hours a day for free. My mom negotiated with Mike to force him to take $5 an hour to cover his gas and tennis balls. At my first practice, he told me, "You are one lucky little dude. If your mom let me have you for free, your ass would have been mine, no questions asked. Now I have to be considerate of her as my client." He laughed hysterically, then turned to a firm face and said, "Let's get to work."

Mike taught me to recognize my strengths and weaknesses. Despite being short and slow on foot, I harnessed my reflexes and ball control thanks to Mike. I needed to learn positioning on the court to limit the angles my opponent could use to hit the ball past me. So he showed me how to stop using unnecessary motion in my swing and to use spins to control the ball with the simplest body motions. He told me that I looked cute with my large swings and dancing footwork, but I was overexerting myself and could do more with less. With these strategies, he was able to open me up to what my father wanted me to get – that I could use tennis as a metaphor for developing other aspects of my life.

Mike took pride in helping me be the best I could be. He said he did so because I was willing to put in the work and take his criticism. "Those two values will help you overcome whatever you face in life," he said.

***

MY LAST YEAR playing baseball was the summer before my sophomore year in high school. We had a traveling team of some of the top talent in the U. City summer league. I made the team because I worked my tail off in practice. I beat out a better athlete for starting second base because our coach appreciated my effort. Our first game of the season in East St. Louis, an area known for violence and poverty and little league sports, brought forth some stories that had all of my coaches fearful as we went across the river. That day I batted last in the batting order, and I got the only hit of the game for our team on my first time at bat.

As I approached first base, the other team threatened me if I tried to make it to second base. "Come on, white boy, you bet not think 'bout goin' to second base." I didn't think anything of it as they were likely just talking shit. Plus, I was hoping to challenge them and prove them wrong. Well, the adults who brought us, primarily our Head Coach Peyton, were concerned enough by the threat that they pulled me from the game as soon as the inning was over. The East St. Louis incident was my first hint that sports were riddled with politics of race and class and even some danger because of that mix.

Sports and the community involve race

My life in sports got complicated later on. Despite being in U. City, a community that emphasized sports and developed many great athletes, students at the high school level often got stuck with subpar coaches such as Coach Crenshaw. Unlike Mr. Stevenson, he struggled with developing talent to its full potential. And soon, we children and parents learned that it would be difficult to remove him from his position without race being a center point for the decision because he was black. Whereas he desperately needed to be replaced with someone who would create the type of disciplined players that would lead to college scholarships, Coach Cren knew very little about molding aspirations and even went so far as to discourage Shando and Gamal from joining the tennis team so they would "focus on basketball."

Like this, he cut off one of the few pathways for inner-city black students to have equitable access to college scholarships. This translated into a city-wide problem. While U. City was great for social development, the public school sports programs suffered from a lack of commitment to developing the natural talent that existed. Too many of my peers ended up being park superstars and not staying in school. Some of them turned to selling drugs instead. The few playground legends who made it to college did so on their own merits. They made it despite the failures of our high school coach.

My father became one of the strong voices pushing for the removal of Coach Crenshaw, especially when he failed to lead us in tennis practice. Cren would just drop off the balls and come back and tell us practice was over. Larry lent an ear to our frustrations and desires and felt moved to do something about it. To many black folks in the community, it appeared as though my dad was using his white privilege to get rid of the black coach. During my senior year, Coach Crenshaw was replaced by Coach Stewart, a black woman math teacher, who played tennis regularly.

My dad also belonged to a school committee designed to replace the U. City principal, another black man. Though beloved by his students, Principal Austin had been thrown into the position and struggled to manage administratively. My father and I clashed about the replacement, a white man from another predominantly black school. He had a stronger background in creating structure but was not empathetic to the student body and did not relate well nor create a welcoming environment as Mr. Austin did. After looking back on it, Larry admitted that Principal Thacker was not the right person to help children stay on a path of education.

I learned from the principal debacle how my father, though he appeared to be choosing a battle based on race, stood for what he believed was best. And although there were mistakes, he was still fighting for the interest of black students. As a young, soon-to-be adult, this was good for me to see. It is a challenge in a society where we are so sensitive to racial issues to remain resolute, especially when you make mistakes or are received in a way that you did not intend.

We are constantly being judged and often without context. Those making judgments are not taking the time to find out the true intentions or circumstances. And sometimes, we have the best intentions and simply screw up. We need the opportunity to keep growing as we learn from our mistakes. It is also easy to feel that, because of whites' destructive history, our place is to only maintain a role of service without stepping up to challenge some of the decisions being made. Finding balance and continuing to develop and make mistakes is what I have found time to appreciate, even though it is also an emotional challenge.

4

Realizing the Extent of My Privilege

After my first encounter with racist cops at the age of 12, it became commonplace for the police to pull my black friends and me over, especially at night as we drove around in my dad's minivan. Never mind that we were a bunch of bright and friendly kids, excelling at school and on various tennis, basketball, and baseball teams.

"Where are you going," "Where did you get this car," "Does the owner, Mr. Mass, know that you are driving his vehicle?" were among the absurd questions the police felt emboldened to ask Shando and Gamal.

I couldn't help but snap back. This often caused my father to have to come and save my ass, again and again. As soon as the police phoned him, he'd light into them, saying, "You woke me up for this crap? I let them drive my car. Were they doing anything wrong to warrant you to stop my son and his friends?" When I wasn't there to help my black friends, the cops would ask them, "So, why does this white man keep saving your ass?"

The grave danger I put us in by smarting off was unacceptable. Sometimes the cops aggressively searched my friends, making them pull out their pants, spread their legs, and jiggle their genitals. By contrast, the cops always seemed very awkward and uncomfortable repeating the commands for me to do the same. It was as if they were either apologetic or hoping I was not the one with the drugs. I would use this privilege to fight back. But while the cops threatened to lock me up due to my mouth, it would be my black friend carted off to jail for having a traffic warrant. With my protestations, these stops could have easily turned into physical assault, or even worse, police shootings.

Walking on the wild side of white privilege

At the age of 16, with the ability to drive, I was able to experience many more examples of the privilege I was afforded and witness, in comparison, the discrimination my friends faced regularly. For me, this was also an age of rebellion – wanting to stick it back to the system that I was just beginning to see as criminal in nature. It was my junior year of high school – the early 90s – and everybody stayed up on the hottest gear. We U. City kids often set trends such as Polo outfits, Tommy Hilfiger rugby shirts, silk shirts, and creased Marithé + François Girbaud jeans with the heavy starch. We felt so highly invested in our look we'd go to bizarre lengths to achieve that style.

My friends and I afforded our love of fresh-white sneaks by taking advantage of the return policy at mall department stores. We'd buy a pair of Reebok Classics only to take them back after two weeks for a new pair. At one point, I returned a pair of barely worn sneakers over 30 times in a year.

Because I was white, no one questioned me. But my black friends didn't have "the complexion for the protection," as comedian Paul Mooney said, and so, I'd return their shoes ranging from size 7 to 14 with no problem. Most of these returns happened within minutes of my friends being denied. After meeting my friends in the mall parking lot, I would take the same pair back to the same person. The fact that my whiteness gave me clearance to return things my black friends couldn't infuriated me all over again.

Racism and revenge at the mall

One time, during the Christmas season of our senior year in high school, Shando needed to exchange two pairs of jeans he was gifted that fit too small for his tall frame. A young white male clerk at Famous Barr helped him complete the exchange, but it was not without unnecessary and seemingly bigoted criticism. Despite the jeans being unworn and folded with tags and stickers on them, the clerk made a disparaging remark about Shando when he walked over to the counter where I was attempting to return a shirt that had clearly been worn many times and was much too large for me.

I had no receipt, and as I walked to the counter, I grabbed a tag from a new $96 rugby shirt off the rack and used it to return the shirt. At the counter, I overheard the racist clerk telling a colleague, "That black guy came to return some pants. He probably wore them down and stunk them up." He didn't know Shando from a can of paint but managed to cast this terrible slander based solely on his race. I suddenly stood tall in my 5'3.5" body and vowed swift revenge for Shando, who hovered in the distance.

"I'm here to return this shirt," I said, pushing the crumpled merchandise toward my clerk, who was also a young white male. "No, I don't have a receipt." The clerk held up the shirt and balked at the visible ring around the collar. I immediately feigned upset and announced, "That ring was around the collar when I bought it!" Without hesitance, the clerk returned the shirt and thanked me for my business. As I pivoted my heels and walked off, I could feel the clerks' eyes staring hard at my back. With my $96 store voucher in hand, I bounced right up to Shando and gave him the most grandiose high-five. We laughed and were glad to see the clerk's look of disgust in plain sight.

Milking my white privilege

Seething about the blatant prejudice we just experienced, we sat in the parking lot and came up with a plot to run schemes using my white privilege as a means of retributive justice. I was still getting used to this level of privilege and was worried that my parents would find out, knowing they taught me to be better than the racist system. But I was upset at the disparity I had witnessed, which was my prevailing emotion at the time.

As we rolled to the next mall, Shando and Quicc whipped out some weed and offered me some. I said 'no' because I worried about how we'd smell inside the stores. Shando suddenly yelled at me, "Man, you white! What are you worried about? This is your world! Now shut the hell up and hit this shit!!" This was my friend since the age of four, so I understood him well. Shando's corruption would never be excused. Instead, his criminality would always be assumed whether he was right or wrong.

Our most lucrative scheme involved us going to the mall and lowering the price of expensive clothing items by ripping off its price tag and replacing it with a smaller priced tag. Being the acceptable white face, I would handle the purchases and meet my black friends back in the car. We'd then head to the next store, and I would return the merchandise using the original price tag while they would continue to switch tags for the next purchase.

At one point, during the Christmas season, we went to four Famous Barr stores a day for three days until we turned that ring around the collar rugby into $2,000 in store vouchers. The following year Nelly joined us. We got so good at the tag-changing scheme that we had schemed one return into roughly $2,000 for each of us by the time the stores caught on.

I have reflected on this experience many times over the years. I remember two prevailing feelings. First, I felt justified for my behavior. I wasn't hurting any humans because the corporation took the hit, and they had other ways to get that profit back. But more importantly for me, it created a flame inside me to use my privilege to the best of my ability to uplift my friends and black folks in general. I did not know how or even if I would be able to achieve it, but I began to approach all of my decisions moving forward, thinking about black empowerment.

Becoming an accomplice to the drug game

Eventually, we grew into men, and I went on to college. During a summer break, I learned that one of my closest friends got kicked out of his mother's house and went missing for a week. When I finally saw him, he had lost a lot of weight because he had barely eaten. My mom let him stay in our family home for a while. He worked a minimum wage job which was good but hardly enough to support himself and a new child on the way. With no diploma or job prospects, my friend dove into the drug trade as a way to boost his earnings and support his family.

Some of my other friends opted to sell drugs as well. And since we were so tight, I often joined them as the driver for their drug runs across the city. Every time, my white skin came in handy. It was natural. While hanging out, they would get calls for drug runs. I would take them for the deliveries because my skin tone reduced our chance of getting caught. In turn, I got a real high out of using my privilege to keep them safe and able to make money. In hot drug areas, my chances of being trailed by the police were nil simply because I'm white. When it came to selling weed, it didn't take long for me to get involved in helping out. Soon, I tapped the trade and gave a bunch of white boys I knew from work access to the product. Ever loyal, I felt like I was genuinely helping my friends, even at the risk of our lives.

Despite being grown-ass men, we'd meet at various friends' houses, where drugs, guns, weed, and alcohol mixed with tons of trash talking and joning (slang for making fun of each other, what people call "roasting" today). "Lil short ass muthafucka," they'd say to me. No matter how wild our exchanges got, I always felt safe in the company of my friends in the room. As I watched some of them stow guns to their belts or take chunks of crack out of their mouth, I reflected on how we all grew up innocently, climbing on jungle gyms and playing dodgeball.

Beyond the crime element, we talked extensively about how rigged the system was and, ultimately, strategies for surviving. "As long as you can continue to get product, don't hold onto it trying to maximize your profits, make the money turnover in the fastest time you can to make a profit," a buddy informed me. That is true in any business. Once innocent boys, we now stood as men trying to figure out how not to be victims of the system. For some, the best idea at the time led us to illicit activity. Yet, in the face of ongoing racism, we all felt vindicated.

Being the only one

I do not want to paint the picture of it all being good in my community interactions as though everyone loved me. I was met with bullying in middle school and, to a lesser degree, in high school. There were those who attempted to push me around at school sometimes because I was white or small or both. I was feisty and often fought back or talked shit right back to them. They also knew Shando was looking out for me, which they tried to use to make me feel weak. "Where's Shando at now?" or "You gonna run and tell Shando?" were the most common replies to attempts to belittle me.

Sometimes when we were out at gatherings or parties and I would see people I attended school with, I would get approached for money. It was known that if we went out and one of my friends didn't have the money to pay their way, I would cover them. Really, my parents covered us all. So other students would try to pressure me as well. When I would say no to their request, "Oh, you'll buy Nelly and Fat E a meal, but I can't get one? I see how you are." I heard in an upset tone as if I had done something wrong. I felt obligated to explain that it was my choice and that they were my friends. They didn't just randomly come to me asking for money.

Many times, when we went to the roller skating rink, parties, and, as we got older, clubs, I was the only one in the room with my skin tone. I got used to the feeling, and it didn't bother me per se. I was conscious of it at all times, though, and I paid attention to the looks my friends and I got. Plenty of times we went out we got talked about and sometimes fights were started with us. Most of that had to do with us being from U City, and others were jealous. It could have been because the ladies were attracted to my friends and not giving the other males the same attention. When it did get to a level of envy, there would always be someone saying something about us being soft because we had a white boy in the crew. Me being a short white boy added to the "soft look."

I was never really scared (or as scared as I maybe should have been at times looking back on it). I did feel somewhat out of place at times and was overly cautious about how I moved. I didn't feel out of place socially because I did enjoy the same music, entertainment, and topics of discussion. I felt like I was invading a space that was comfortable for others not to be bothered with the likes of me given the history of my culture. I never came close to experiencing the same apprehension that black folks often feel being the only one in the room of white folks. Though, I believe that being in those settings did help me empathize somewhat to their level of discomfort.

Lastly, when my friends took me to their family's neighborhood in the inner city, I got a lot of stares from the neighbors. It would take multiple visits over time for the neighborhood folks to feel comfortable with me coming around. I understood why. I appreciated why they would be cautious. Hell, I could be the police or willing to report to the police. Another reason for their concern is that if I ended up being harmed, that meant someone would get locked up, innocent or not. Also, I could be judging their living conditions and feel like I was better than them because I had more and could go back home.

I would do my best to acknowledge any of that if it was brought to me. I would also acknowledge what I recognized about my people's history and current decision-making. I wanted them to know I had a level of understanding in an attempt to ease them to me being around. No one should feel discomfort in their own community from an outside visitor. I met so many people that did not want to leave the inner city because it was their only place of comfort. Of course, my friends would let the community know that I belonged with them. Through all of my daily experiences, I remember staring at my ceiling before bed each night from middle school through high school appreciating what I had while hoping and praying that others would soon be able to have the same. I still pray for that to this day.

5

Shooting to the Top with Nelly

In 1999, I graduated college and started a career in banking. Still driven to help black folk, my mission was to leverage my expertise in finance to empower black enterprise. I had just purchased my own home in South City, St. Louis, and was seeing my career path come into focus, until that day in August 2000. I was visiting with my mother when suddenly I got a call that would change my life. "I got my first million-dollar check," said Nelly. "Let's do this," he yelped. Having been friends since before our freshman year of high school, Nelly and I knew exactly what he meant.

His debut album *Country Grammar* was hitting #1 on the Billboard charts for the third week in a row and had just gone 2 times platinum. Nelly needed a trusted partner to help manage his business ideas aimed at empowering as many friends and family as possible. Money-savvy and with the complexion to open key doors, he chose me for this historic moment. "I want to open a shoe store. A nightclub. A community basketball and fitness center," Nelly once told me. "Quit your job Fam. I'll pay you that bank salary and buy you a car," he said. I put in my two-week notice the very next day.

I called my grandmother, Bubby, to tell her the news. She flat out said, "I don't think that's such a good idea." But in my heart, I knew Nelly's offer was one I couldn't refuse. All my life I wanted to realize Martin Luther King's dream of creating an equal America. With Nelly, I saw the chance to build an empire and introduce myself and my goals to influential people who could expand our impact. It wasn't about the money, but what we could do with it to make a difference.

In August of 2000, I got started. My first order of business was setting up a new office in the Central West End, gathering a team, and steering the boat of Nelly's start-up dreams. His pioneering rap group the St. Lunatics had an existing business and in 2001, they looked to me to restructure and advance their operations as well. As I turned the key to our new office, I paused to reflect on where our friendship took off.

In the 9th grade, Nelly, Shando, and others invited me to be a part of a large crew called FOTI, named after Digital Undergrounds' legendary hit "Freaks of the Industry." As FOTI, we spent hours freestyling, cracking jokes, dressing fly, and chasing girls. At our school, Nelly was the most talented person - a football, baseball and basketball player. Without a doubt, if you wanted to be the best at anything, you had to beat Nelly at it. At the age of 19, we all saw that Nelly had a talent for rap and had something special. He was super funny and mixed that playful, country-crooning with gangsta spitting that would go on to make him one of the best-selling rappers in the world. He possessed that *it* factor to the point of rubbing it off on everyone he met, including me.

Race threatened to derail our plans

Fast-forward to 2001, my main focus was helping Nelly pursue his entrepreneurial endeavors outside of his music and touring. However, what I didn't see coming would prove to be kryptonite to our plans. At every turn, societal and industry racism lurked like a vulture, waiting to clip our wings even before we could take off. In my effort to keep us abound, I developed a serious case of The White Savior Syndrome and began trying to save the day in numerous, short-sighted ways. We were so overwhelmed by the amount of success Nelly had. This, combined with our youthful ignorance, made for many classes in the school of hard knocks.

While I took responsibility for much of what went wrong, I realized that once caught in the system of Hollywood capitalism, it's hard to escape with your full dignity. And, as much as Nelly and I wanted to manifest all of his dreams, I learned the hard way that having money and talent is not enough to override external racism and internal cultural differences.

The hometown racism stung the worst

From day one, Nelly envisioned owning a nightclub in downtown St. Louis, a historical business zone struggling to reclaim its glory days. The overarching idea was to employ as many people as possible through his ventures and the night club world fit perfectly into this world. The planned upscale venue would cater to lounge-goers and the urban hip-hop crowd interested in different genres of entertainment from pop to reggae. After some searching, we found a spacious club inside a building located on Locust St. and 11th St. An old convent, the rest of the building was overrun by birds, so we had a good chance of securing it with the hopes of revival. Within weeks, a team of experts in real estate construction and restaurants, and I finalized the contract to purchase the building and sought the necessary signatures to obtain a liquor license for the club.

The only thing we needed were neighboring building and apartment owners to support us with their signature. *This should be achievable right?* Or so we thought. The space was already a nightclub that recently closed. So off we went to gain support. Sadly, it was one excuse after another. A white woman in charge of one of the housing communities said she "didn't move downtown to have all that noise at all times of the night." Later, two white male owners of neighboring buildings said they didn't want to "rock the boat" and would sign only if others signed. They were both from out of town and did admit they were shocked at how racist St. Louis was despite it being over 50 percent black. For example, one of them mentioned how Mayor Francis Slay allocated $22 million in funds for street repair and infrastructure, yet $2 million went to black areas while the other $20 million went to the smaller, majority-white wards. Hearing this turned my frustration into determination.

Five months went by of us beating the pavement and nothing. Left and right, we were denied signatures by irrevocable negative attitudes towards "urban crowds." My white skin had proven no bridge for Nelly and the folks he planned to empower through this club. Soon, we were forced to give up. What stung the worst happened two months later. The building opened up as a nightclub for pop and electronic music.

So my team and I visited the Mayor's office where Slay's head of urban development told us how thankful they were to have Nelly represent and promote the city. Yet in the same breath, she suggested we lease some "great" land north of Downtown in a dilapidated manufacturing building far away from other businesses or residents. "Did they think that we are that stupid not to see what they are doing?" Nelly fumed. After a year of attempting to get

Nelly a nightclub, I realized that for the first time in my life, I could leave St. Louis for good. "Who needs a place that doesn't welcome what we brought to the table because of the 'black element' that comes with it?" I said to myself. "Was this 2001 or 1901?"

Early mistakes in my approach

While I had Nelly's best interest at heart, I made decisions early on that opened up for a lack of trust. First, he told me to buy myself a car, on his dollar. He suggested a BMW SUV or something similar. I chose a Chevy Monte Carlo and chose to use the rest of that money to hire a college friend, D Denham to support me in building the Nelly businesses. I felt it was necessary and a better use of funds, but Nelly was disappointed. He had his reasons for wanting me to get a nicer ride because I represented him, and I chose to handle it my way without discussing my decision with him.

Shortly thereafter, I joined Nelly's management team with the intention to reduce his cost of my staff and me and help the management stabilize their operations. Once again, with so much happening at the time, we made moves quickly. Nelly's desire was to keep what I was doing separate from his music career. With me on the inside of his career, establishing his entrepreneurial endeavors became easier to promote. But the path that I took did not build trust. I arrogantly relied on the bond we built from our childhood not recognizing the importance of this being the chance Nelly had with riches that could set his family up for generations. My lack of awareness opened the door for questions about my trustworthiness down the road. Given how shaky trust can be especially when coming from an environment of instability to a large amount of fame and fortune, this became my Achilles heel.

With all that came of Nelly's success, his desire was never to get deeply involved in the business operations. I wanted him involved at a much greater level especially given his position as the ultimate decision-maker. While operating without his full attention, Ali and Yomi, the two with harmful intent inside our group, stayed in his ear. They were both jealous of those of us who had success in our roles and took advantage of the opportunity to create dissension. In the end, these attempts to bring me and others downplayed a major role in why I left the organization and split ways with Nelly.

Reflections on my white savior syndrome

In the early days of my time with Nelly, I first saw my job as an opportunity to save his team and the St. Lunatics' team from making many mistakes given their lack of experience having such levels of cash flow. I wanted to teach them how to budget and evaluate investments properly. I did it out of love, and also in a very arrogant, white savior type of way. Whenever anyone on the team struggled or faced challenges, I would step in and sometimes take over, thinking I could save the day.

Whether it was for an event, negotiating a contract for an endorsement or clothing line, I ended up getting involved in everything. I didn't even bother keeping a calendar. The opportunities at the door were so plentiful, I could only manage what was in front of me at the moment. This was the direct byproduct of being the white man in the black room, erroneously thinking that I had either the right answers or that I could use my privilege to be the a**hole saying, "no, no, no," knowing that my voice would be respected.

Nelly would tell me to let people make mistakes, which was a philosophy deeply rooted in a black cultural approach to life and learning. He especially told me to let them create their way. This was a struggle for me internally because I wanted others to win – if only they listened to my advice. Looking back, I realize this was a flawed mentality. But, with limited understanding at that time, it was all I had to go on.

Industry white supremacy & exploitation

Early on, as Nelly navigated his record deal with Universal, it became clear that he would transform the rap game forever. After selling more than 7.7 million of the *Country Grammar* album by 2002, every label in America started looking for their Nelly. His crooning sound spread like a musical wildfire, igniting an era of city-pride, club hits, colorful fashion and melodious, sing-songy hooks across the hip-hop industry. Hits such as *Dilemma* and *Hot in Herre* from his second album *Nellyville* rode the top of the charts for the longest time. No other artist had achieved this accomplishment with two songs on top of the charts since the Bee Gees. Nelly defined a whole era of free-spirited ambition and feel-good music, achieving success that is rare in the diversity of its reach. One could easily argue that Nelly and the St. Lunatics absolutely spawned the future of hip-hop, laying the roots that birthed stars such as T-Pain, Flo Rida and many others.

To the old white male executives, however, Nelly and the Lunatics were just another opportunity to capitalize on for their personal profit. The old white male mentality controlled the decisions made in the hip-hop industry, from the type of songs produced to their messages and marketing of black artists. Their decisions were all based on analytics, not the needs of the customers to be elevated, healed and whole. Artists were mere products and their fans, mere numbers in a spreadsheet.

To me, the most exploitative aspect of the industry was how labels structured their agreements, using artists as chess pieces who had virtually no control. The result was nothing less than pimping the artists who bartered their equity for a chance at fame. Artists would typically get about 15% of the revenues until they were proven money-makers. From this tiny percentage, the artist paid for all of the costs of producing and promoting their music.

Sure, the label takes risks with production and promotion, but the 85/15 deal, where the artist's 15% repays for every cost is a dangerous deal. To keep artists motivated by this inherently exploitative arrangement, labels offered artists trinkets, dangled like carrots before hungry rappers: material gifts, parties, travel, and a platform for fame. Luckily, Nelly had what it took to squeeze personal wealth from this risky formula, enough to invest in himself and others. But the pimping culture left me sick and tired.

When Hollywood called Nelly to make the song "#1" for the soundtrack to *Training Day* starring Denzel Washington, we were geeked. He was paid a hefty sum of cash and gifted a Rolls Royce. But Nelly's accountant and I kept thinking, "Sorry, we'll take the cash." Why dangle the car?

It reminded me of the birthday party in Vegas that Universal threw for Nelly after he was signed. They flew out all of his friends and filled the room with alcohol. The white executives were standing by and watching us dance with the girls and pop bottles. It all went with the pimp game. I kept thinking we could have thrown our own party and made some money from sponsors if we wanted to. But, like pimps, the execs held the lion's share of the cash, while Nelly's talent paid for their future wealth. They probably even put that party into their marketing budget and recouped the expense anyway. That's the way it was.

The executives maintained a financial model that ultimately promoted music that fuels the destruction of the black family and community. It's easy to blame stars like Nelly for perpetuating pathologies and stereotypes that inspire young black boys and girls to indulge in sex, drugs, and material pursuits; however, this type of self-destructive culture is only the message tolerated by white label owners.

Russell Simmons, P. Diddy and Master P all created their black-owned labels but still had to rely on white institutions for airtime and distribution. All too often, degrading songs are pushed through the airways by white capitalists, and the artists are incentivized to do whatever it takes to survive. This means creating drama and violence that feeds self-hatred in the black community. While money is gained, the true beauty and diversity of black people are willfully and effectively suppressed. Then, and still now, this aspect of the industry disgusts and infuriates me deep in my soul.

Racism landed us a second-class investment with NASCAR

In 2002, Nelly released his second album "Nellyville" with the hit "Hot in Herre" that single-handedly put him in the pop music hall of fame. As the record scorched club floors worldwide it also opened the gate for business deals from new, unlikely industries and suitors. The following year, one of the management team members, Courtney B, had the vision to get involved in the multi-billion dollar NASCAR racing industry. The domain of mostly white men, NASCAR was essentially the antithesis of hip-hop and had dusted numerous blacks from Julius Erving to Jackie Joyner-Kersey who had tried and failed to break in. Still, the fast cars and the chance to add more color to the sport piqued our interest. Most exciting, we'd be primarily supporting a promising black driver, Tim Woods, who in turn would promote Nelly's clothing lines Vokal and Apple Bottoms.

After a few talks with Tim's team however, we realized we didn't have the funding needed to make a deal. I was devastated. We bought a trailer and paid for our logos to be everywhere but were short a few million dollars to run a full team. For a moment, we thought we had a lifeline when Michael Warmack convinced us to partner with Billy Ballew Motorsports (for whom Michael was the agent) out of North Carolina. We agreed to transfer ownership of our race truck and trailer to Billy while Michael was going to find the rest of the endorsers.

Shortly before the big Darlington 200 truck event, Billy's team said it didn't have the money to meet us halfway. Trying to salvage the plans, I made payments from Nelly's money after being threatened to be sued by Michael Warmack who I feared would scream to the media. Nelly's second album was doing great. I was scared of the bad publicity as more opportunities came our way. Right before Darlington 200, Billy's team backed out of allowing our black driver Tim to race. Stuck with a branded truck but not the rider, we watched hundreds of thousands of dollars go down the drain.

Later that year, Michael Warmack came to us about purchasing Billy's facilities and equipment outright. I had the lawyers look at the contracts and it all seemed to be intact, but shortly after we made the financial commitment, the assets were gone, Warmack had conned us out of our money and trailer. Here we were in the whitest sport, full of country boys who ultimately showed us no regard. In the end, no one was surprised and felt that they needed to run to our aid. Given that our crew was black, this betrayal hurt even more.

Still, with a sliver of hope, a new friend and agent helped Nelly reposition himself to become a NASCAR team owner. Finally, Nelly had established the Atlanta-based Vokal Racing Team. And then "the swipe" happened. In 2003, BET's Uncut premiered Nelly's *Tip Drill* video. It featured a symphony of half-naked women dancing and that infamous moment when Nelly took a credit card and swiped it down a dancer's backside. That one swipe shook the world. So much so, the women of Spelman College in Atlanta protested Nelly's arrival to a bone marrow drive they had partnered with him to host. The news made headlines instantly and turned away potential NASCAR sponsors for the team. Since sponsors were so important to having a team, that was the end of the NASCAR dream. In the end, it was this striking act of sexism and internalized racism that hurt us the most.

Internal issues arise to challenge Apple Bottoms

After experiencing success with his clothing line Vokal for men, Nelly sought to launch a clothing line for women. In 2002, Nelly, and the Vokal team, led by his friend Yomi Martin launched Apple Bottoms. With its signature decaled jeans for women with full derrieres, the brand excited me instantly. Nelly then hired Leslie Ungar to be President of Apple Bottoms. She was a sales rep at Vokal and had grown up in her father's clothing manufacturing business. A white woman with a pretty smile and a go-getter mentality, Leslie and I became a couple shortly into this process. As Nelly invested in Apple Bottoms with his own money, we had set a goal for managing a budget he provided and raising outside capital that was needed. Apple Bottoms became an instant hit in the hip hop culture and required more of an investment than we originally thought.

The winter after launching, orders erupted. As we moved operations from St. Louis to LA, the company needed to find financing fast. Unfortunately, Yomi, who was sore about his smaller role in Apple Bottoms than in Vokal, spoke to potential investors behind our backs and told them that Leslie and I were going to be replaced soon due to Nelly's dissatisfaction with us. He told investors that we were blamed for costing Nelly more than he wanted to spend. The reality was that we underestimated how fast the line would grow and we could not afford people with experience in key positions. When the investors learned from us that Yomi had twisted the story, they did not want to be involved in such a messy situation for fear that their money would be lost in the St. Louis culture of backstabbery.

Differences in cultures affect business

Leslie turned to her father who had recently partnered with a private financier from the fashion industry. We entered into a manufacturing partnership that exposed the difference in cultures. Our financier agreed to pay for the manufacturing until they realized that many of our buyers were cash buyers in the inner-city. Ultimately, it was distrust in our hip-hop market that hurt us the most. Our financiers did not understand the cash buyer market nor the trends in hip hop culture. They were certainly not convinced of the popularity of our jeans. They based their purchase power on the credit of the stores we would sell to and since our stores paid in cash, they began to backtrack paying for our goods to be produced.

After constant negotiations, they began to pay for many of the items, but a few orders were left unfulfilled. Naturally, we threatened to sue. By the time this got back to Nelly who for the most part stayed out of it, all he was told and heard was that Leslie's father screwed us over and we had to sue our partners. Now, it appeared to Nelly that Leslie was unqualified and that I looked like her protector rather than his. At the same time, we had finally turned the corner with the volume of sales that we were in a position to make a profit, but it was too little too late.

It didn't matter that my team and I were bringing on a new group of successful entrepreneurs in film, entertainment, printing, and merchandising to help take every facet of Nelly's endeavors to a higher level. It didn't matter that a Samsung-backed financier that bought into FUBU and Coogi was offering to repay half of Nelly's investment in advance and a much better split than either FUBU or Coogi received. The leader of the Samsung-backed group still valued Leslie but Nelly wanted nothing to do with her. These entrepreneurs met with Nelly, and he shared his lost trust in Leslie and me. Yomi then brought a licensing deal to the table and Nelly decided to go forward with it. Leslie was fired, I quit and one of the employees from the group of entrepreneurs replaced me.

As I look back on that time, Nelly and I were both blinded by our own ambition and others fed off of it. Underneath it all, we didn't realize that my white savior syndrome needed to be addressed. Leslie was also very difficult to work with because she brought many of the attributes of white culture capitalism. Everything was met with such a sense of urgency. Mistakes were seen as catastrophes rather than learning opportunities, and she wanted to micromanage everybody's job. Add into the fact that Leslie and I never should have married.

The St. Lunatic crew was already a family-like environment. She really didn't want to participate. For her, it was strictly business, which brought forth a heightened level of emotions between her, Nelly and me. Ali and Yomi saw a chance to undercut what Leslie and I were working on. Nelly wanted to protect me from my mistakes, I wanted to show him that I was capable of catapulting his business empire, and Leslie wanted to prove that she could fulfill her dream to create a successful clothing line. While all of us made great decisions along with our blunders, Apple Bottoms' lack of success ultimately became my hardest pill to swallow.

6

Meeting The African Hebrew Israelites

During my college days, a close childhood friend Topher (short for Christopher, pronounced Topha) and our buddy Dedrick, challenged me to stop eating beef and pork. It was 1995 and they recently cut these red meats from their diet. "You will feel so much better, trust me," Topher bragged. A life-long meat eater, I flat out told them 'No!"

I even started quoting Eddie Murphy's *Boomerang*, "I love evrathang on the pig from the roota to the toota!" Seeing my resistance, they waged a bet. If I gave up beef and pork for one month, then I would never want to eat it again, they hypothesized. *Not a chance!* I thought. As such, I agreed to fork over $100 to both Topher and Dedrick if in fact they were right. Convinced I would win, I tossed in milk as well and even though I ate cereal twice a day, nearly every day. In my mind I thought, *Have my pulled pork sandwich ready!*

To my surprise, I noticed a big difference in my life almost immediately. My snotty nose cleared up. Yes, I still had a snot nose at the age of 20. Best of all, my stomach stopped hurting like it did after I ate beef and pork. Finally, on day 30, I withdrew the $200 out of my bank and brought it straight to campus. Topher laughed yet felt so proud of my progress. Since then, I have yet to eat beef and pork again. Little did I know that my dietary change would pave the way for an epic life transformation, as well. This new diet led me to the African Hebrew Israelites, a lively community and daring group of black vegans who believe they are the descendants of the original Hebrews of Israel.

The very next year, I cut out chicken. And in 1997, turkey was out. On my 25th birthday, I gave myself until age 30 to become totally vegan. Then one day, I ran into Eternity Deli, a Hebrew Israelite-owned soul vegan restaurant down the street from the bank I worked at in North County. I walked in and ordered a gyro sandwich made with an in-house meat substitute called seitan. The food was so delicious, I soon found myself there twice a week ordering everything from the mouth-watering collard greens to mock ribs and soy mac and cheese. Over the next few months, the staff and I had many eye-opening conversations about the health benefits of the food and how the U.S. was unhealthy and violent by nature. I grew increasingly interested in the Israelite community and felt like the savory food and conversation was a gateway to my elevation. Soon, I realized my goal of going vegan hovered even closer within reach.

As serendipity had it, I met an older black man in my office at the bank who told me he was an African Hebrew. We sparked up a work friendship. He told me that the Hebrew teachings we call the Torah were written by his ancestors and most of the slave trade captured African Hebrews. This made immediate sense to me for two reasons. First, the fact that melanated humans occupied Northeastern Africa where Israel is located seemed right. Secondly, the practices of my white Jewish and Christian folks did not match the teachings of the bible as much as what I witnessed from those who we oppressed. I remained open and eager for our numerous follow-up talks.

During my undergrad years, Topher and I shared a ride to Saint Louis U. together. He and I had many conversations about the design of the world we live in and how that impacted communities. Topher being Mike's best friend, and me being Shando's, we were connected and cherished the fact that we had known each other since I was kindergarten age. Many times, our conversations included Mike or Shando in the discussion. We examined the impacts of racism, how to repair the harm, and the effects of capitalism and consumerism on America and specifically the black communities. These daily discussions about the world inspired me to seek to impact change on a macro level. I thought – how could I do the most with my time and energy?

In 2000, I left banking to join Nelly. I soon opened operations into an old warehouse in the well-to-do Central West End and we converted the space into cubicles, a conference room and meeting areas. This is where we ventured into bigger and bigger deals on behalf of Nelly. I helped run the merchandise with Topher and then Shando and planned exciting things for the brand. Surprisingly, Eternity Delhi moved in a few blocks away. In St. Louis, there were no other vegan options. I only knew how to cook toast and grits - albeit pipin' hot and tasty grits! Thanks to Eternity, I ate good and often, and soon, I met more people who ran the Deli and who belonged to the larger community of African Hebrew Israelites. Through camaraderie and delicious cuisine, they made my shift towards a vegan diet seem more achievable. They also inspired me to imagine a world capable of new and better things.

Within months of Nelly's career taking off, his uncle, Amikham, began to visit us regularly, driving down from Chicago. Amikham, I was happy to learn, was a member of the African Hebrew Israelites of Jerusalem community. We would have the most beautiful conversations about health, life in America, race, religious writings, and any topic under the sun. The African Hebrew Israelites originated at the end of the 19th century in the U.S. and branched out to many different sects. His community called themselves the Kingdom of Yah (KOY).

"In 1966, its Chicago-born leader Ben Ammi Ben-Israel received a holy vision of the angel Gabriel calling the black descendants of the Biblical Israelites to return to the Promised Land and establish the Kingdom of God. The next year, Ben Ammi overcame tremendous anxiety about this vision and successfully led 350 African Americans from Chicago to Liberia, West Africa. In 1969, the first members of the Kingdom finally reached the Promised Land in Israel."
(Taken from https://africanhebrewisraelitesofjerusalem.com/our-leadership/ben-ammi/)

Because they view the Bible quite literally, they do not recognize the white interpretation of Christianity or Judaism, but rather, consider themselves born-again children of the ancient black Hebrews that were exiled from the Land of Israel after the Roman invasion. As a result, the Black Hebrew Israelites have been accused of being anti-white. There are many groups or tribes that recognize themselves to be Israelites. While there are many similarities among these groups, they may disagree on how they practice, how they interpret the teachings of the Scriptures, and how they choose to communicate their vision with the outside world, especially white Jews and Christians. This is no different than how there are different sects of Jews or Christians.

In 1969, the first members of that community entered Israel and laid the foundation for their vision of "God's Kingdom" on Earth. They were held in the airport for many days and eventually given land in Dimona near a nuclear plant. After initially being received as new immigrants, by 1971 they saw their status revoked. There without legal protection, the African Hebrew Israelites endured cyclical attempts at deportation, banishment from national educational and health care systems and repeated attacks on their character.

Instead of retreating however, the Hebrews used adversity as motivation, building schools and health care and economic infrastructures to provide for themselves. One of their overall goals is to live autonomously, grow their own food and practice their own culture. They are a peaceful people living mainly in Dimona, Israel, hundreds of them in the Village of Peace with hundreds more living throughout the city as a whole.

After many talks, Amikham encouraged me to go to Israel to visit the Village of Peace. Despite my Jewish roots, I lacked interest in Israel up until that moment. My father refused to go as long as Israel hadn't made peace with and repaired the harm caused to the Palestinian people. "If Larry wouldn't go, then neither would I," I reasoned. Soon though, the more I learned about the KOY, the more mesmerized I became about going and supporting their mission of spreading the idea of peace and health by reconnecting to – not destroying – the planet.

Needing to personally heal

In early 2003, I moved full-time to Los Angeles to set up a presence for Nelly and his rap group, the St. Lunatics, in Hollywood. We planned as well to launch operations for Apple Bottoms. It all seemed very promising at the time. Nelly's career was reaching unbelievable heights. I recently got engaged to the Apple Bottoms President, Leslie, and we married during the summer of that year. As if life couldn't get any better, my good friend Mike and his wife Satrice moved out to LA to work with me and Leslie. My best friend Shando was a call away and ran the merchandise with Nelly's crew on tour.

By early 2004, everything changed. Nelly and I parted ways. I made some critical mistakes, and sadly, new partners I sought to bring into our camp turned on me by trying to fire Leslie. Our quick rise in the industry didn't help in the process. Shooting up into stardom found us completely unskilled at playing the ruthless Hollywood game while protecting our personal loyalties at the same time. The only ones who stuck with me were Shando, Mike and the Jordan Family, and in the end, they gained only a pittance for all the hard work they invested in the merchandise sales and Apple Bottoms.

My relationship with Leslie soon soured and we split due to mutual dissatisfaction. I moved in with Mike and Satrice. The next year and a half were rough to say the least. Not only was I negotiating a settlement with Nelly, but my loss of friends and failed marriage also crushed my heart under a boulder of unhappiness. Day and night, regret sickened my soul while anger towards those who sabotaged me burned a pain in my spirit that threatened to destroy me. My suffering became so unbearable, I turned to carbs, snacks and desserts to bring back my joy. I had packed on 30 pounds when I reached out to my grandmothers, Mimi and Bubby, for some much-needed support.

Amid the fall-out, Mimi (my mom's mom) gifted me a book from her Yoga and Hindu studies that taught me to use my mind to observe body and emotions and to learn from this self-reflection. Bubby (my dad's mom) asked if I wanted to go to Israel with her and friends from her retirement community. I would be the only one under the age of 60 and Bubby the oldest at 84. Seeing I had nothing to look forward to in LA, I thought why not? The vacation would be two weeks: 2 days of flights and 12 days of a guided tour. Although Israel was in the news for a lot of violence lately, Bubby's enthusiasm gave me confidence. If she wasn't afraid, why should I be?

I called Amikham immediately. "You have to spend at least three of those days in Dimona," he pleaded. I took this idea back to Bubby and she immediately shot it down. "No way do we have time to veer from the tour. Twelve days is already not long enough to experience Israel." We debated back and forth for days until finally, I successfully won her buy-in for a half-day visit to Dimona. At the midpoint of the trip, when the rest of the group went to the Dead Sea, she and I would sneak off and visit the Village of Peace.

Going to Israel

When I arrived in the Holy Land, an amazing feeling overcame me. I sensed something different about the air and the energy in Israel. A friend who had recently returned from visiting Europe spoke of the feeling of permanence whereas the States felt like a facade. I agreed and realized that in Israel there is also a level of connection to the earth that vibrates everywhere. That connection was reflected in the freshness of the foods and the natural flavors that burst through when eating the fruits and vegetables grown in the land. And perhaps, this spiritual vibration explained why European Jews refused to stop fighting for control of this precious land. Coming off my divorce and hard times in LA, I opened my heart

Race for What?

and let Israel begin to heal me, even if it meant dealing with privileged white Jews. Being with the KOY community would only enhance my quest which I believed could become a spiritual renewal for me.

Bubby was initially turned off by my wanting to visit the community. I boasted about the Kingdom's focus on health, shared community lifestyle, promotion of peace and building a stronger connection to the planet. But she and the gang couldn't see past the question of polygamy. Men marrying multiple wives is a common practice among the African Hebrew Israelites who consider it "divine marriage." The old white folks felt strongly that women could not be truly happy in this type of marital arrangement. Never mind that many monogamous couples struggle to attain that happiness. Day by day, they questioned me about it, becoming increasingly judgmental. "It sounds like a cult to me JD. If you're not careful, you could end up like one of Jim Jones' followers," Bubby warned.

Still, Bubby possessed a vivacious and curious spirit, so some part of her was willing to take the journey to KOY with an open mind. My determination and excitement eventually won her over. Halfway into our trip, my dear friend Amikham arranged for Bubby and me to be picked up in Jerusalem by a young brother named Yair and Amikham's wife Shadayah. Anticipation trickled from the crown of my head to the tip of my toes. And for the full hour-and-a-half long trip to Dimona, a sense of newness washed over me.

Yair drove the car while I sat in the passenger seat. He calmly and proudly explained to me how his family immigrated from the U.S. to Israel and raised him in a unique way. Children are taught to value relationships with each other and with the planet and let that guide their growth and development. We were both in our late 20s and entrepreneurs. Needless to say, we hit it off. His goal was to provide structure to youth to inspire their development in business and I totally dug that coming from my background in business. Bubby sat on edge in the back with Shadayah, discussing the roles and treatment of the women in the Kingdom. As we got closer to the village, my racing thoughts about the peace we humans are truly capable of found a home in the good company of Yair and Shadayah.

Suddenly, I peered up and saw "Welcome to the Village of Peace." This invitation was proudly displayed on a long metal sign that formed the front facade of the sprawling metal posts and gate. Past the entrance, I witnessed the spread of single-story, apartment-style housing - arranged in five rows, forming somewhat of a U shape. At the center of the U was an open space for gatherings, games and a basketball court. Among the houses, the Israelites converted building spaces into a small grocery store, an ice cream and prepared food spot, a large dining hall, multi-use gathering spaces, a computer center, and a library. Across their village stood their school that catered to children ages four to 18.

Bubby and I were invited to a small relaxation space to enjoy a freshly prepared meal. They served us a savory plant-based meal prepared from scratch: Sauteed kale greens, soy mac and cheese, and a seitan pot roast with gravy. The side romaine salad with fresh cucumbers and tahini dressing topped it all off. With our bellies full and spirits happy, Bubby and I talked, laughed and opened our eyes even more.

One of the Princes, Nasik Emmanuel, joined us to chaperone us on our visit. He spoke to Bubby mainly about the political climate of Israel and KOY's commitment to building relationships with Israel, the Middle East and Africa. Following our meal, Nasik led Bubby and me around the village on foot. Prior to our visit, the KOY community was informed of our coming and that I was involved in Nelly's career.

I wasn't the only special guest. A small group of English journalists and filmmakers buzzed around to produce a story about the KOY. We all planned to meet later at one of the halls to see a private musical performance which I was thrilled to see. Earlier on my trip, I talked with many white Jews about the "Black Hebrews" and every time I mentioned them, their eyes would widen. Everyone knew the Hebrews for creating beautiful music. And that was indeed the goal of the KOY sound - to create uplifting and positive spiritual music that humanized their presence in the homeland.

As Nasik Emmanuel took us around, he explained how they ended up in Dimona. The Israeli government was not welcoming to the Israelites at first. When the first Israelites arrived in the Holy Land in 1969, they came through the Law of Return. The next year, the Law of Return was amended to say that in order to return and become a citizen you must be born of a Jewish mother or converted by an approved rabbi.

At the time, the European Jews who were – and still are – occupying the land did not want the black Israelites in the country. The white officials finally settled on sending the Israelites to Dimona, full of small, abandoned apartments and located near a nuclear plant. This was to be the African Israelites' temporary dwelling. The Israeli government only wanted to allow them temporary structures because they still hoped to remove the returnees. As the community grew, however, they began to renovate and expand the housing, helping Dimona flourish and grow. After negotiations with leaders of the Israelites, Israel's government allowed them to build permanent structures, but the Hebrews were forced to cover the new parts with tarps that made them appear temporary.

All the racism the black Hebrews wished to escape in the U.S., they found in abundance in Israel, Nasik shared with us. The Israelites struggled to receive compensation for their work in white Jewish establishments. Then out of nowhere, planes began spraying mysterious chemicals over their land, in some instances causing health problems for the youth that would be long lasting. Often, the black Israelites were refused access to social services. Banned, rejected and threatened, the government of Israel even offered the community money to leave.

Despite the intentional attempts to harm and dissuade the Israelites, Nasik mainly told us success stories about the growth and development of the community. The school system they created continued to be a site of great pride. We ventured to visit a third-grade classroom. I was happy to see that the students looked healthy and engaged and were being taught about the local plant life. The plants' role in providing life to humans and animals was just as important as taking care of the plants, they learned. Therefore, the victory over racism seemed at least partially clear because, despite extreme struggles, the Israelites managed to raise bright-eyed children who were gaining a higher quality of education.

Eye-opening moment of humanity

There was one moment, I'll never forget. I realized that I urgently needed to use the restroom so I asked Nasik where I could go. He turned to me and said, "Go through any door and use the restroom," and simply pointed to the homes as we walked by. I completely ignored his offer of hospitality which was foreign to me. So, we kept walking until the prince stopped and said, "Didn't you say you had to use it?"

I nodded uncomfortably as we stood in front of a short walkway leading up to someone's home. "Well go inside and use it," he said. Nervous, I tip-toed slowly up to the door and went to knock on it. Nasik snapped, "I did not say knock! I said go inside and use the restroom. We haven't locked our doors in the close to forty years we've been here."

I peeked my head inside the door, and I heard a welcoming woman's voice, "C'mon in baby, what you need? Food, water, the restroom?" "The restroom and some water would be nice," I replied. You could have pinched me because, at this point, I realized I had entered a level of peace unimaginable to me in the States. After I used the restroom and drank the water, I thanked the woman graciously.

After that, Bubby and I were looking forward to seeing the choir and musicians waiting for us, when another unforgettable moment instantly unfolded. A small girl, no more than three years old, ran around a corner and right past us. Nasik said, "You going to the park?" She kept running, making happy little sounds. Bubby and I looked around for adults who we assumed anxiously watched the girl. Nasik told us not to worry. "There are more eyes on her than we could see," he said. "For our children, the entire village is their home. They learn that as soon as they are old enough to walk." Bubby and I were pleasantly amazed.

Alas, we made it to the concert. In a word, it was beautiful. Over ten individual singers, three groups, and a forty-plus member choir performed spiritual, jazz and R&B-style music. I nearly cried as everyone from young children to gray-bearded elders crooned about The Creator, love, life and peace. I was surprised that Amikham hadn't told me that Shadayah was one of the lead vocals with an amazing vocal range.

Fully energized, Bubby and I headed to a recording studio located just outside of the village, after the concert. I met with Shadayah, a few singers and producers of the Kingdom sound to discuss the goal of creating and distributing music as well as other projects being developed. Soon, the time to go back to Bubby's main trip drew near. On our way out of the KOY, Bubby turned to Nasik Emmanuel and said, "You know if anyone can bring peace to this region it's going to be you." To hear her say that just made my year. I truly felt in my heart that I found a home for my idea of how we should live life. The Village of Peace, in my eyes, truly lived up to its name hanging on the sign above the main entrance. And Bubby's approval seemed like a major milestone for both of us.

Bubby beamed with excitement to tell her friends on the trip everything she had experienced. Sadly, they shot her down fast. "Yes, but they have multiple wives." Bubby explained that not all families practiced this structure and that the wives involved share a great respect for one another. Shadayah actually chose Amikham's second wife and the potential third wife that the family considered.

Shadayah explained it like this: American structure creates a family that leans on hired help and the school system to raise their children. At the Village of Peace, people make long-term commitments to being a family and support each other in raising the children. That was a fundamental difference between the Western mentality and the Kingdom's approach. The old ladies on the tour bus poked fun at Bubby, saying she drank the Kool-Aid.

Bubby then turned to me and said, "You know Jesse, Jews can be so stubborn sometimes." I agreed and we both laughed.

For me, polygamy or monogamy was not really the issue. Neither work when the involved parties are not committed to the process and to each other, while they work well when the approach and commitment are the right fit. As I thought about "the family structure," it is designed by each family differently to suit their needs and desires. I chose to be open to new knowledge of this structure because at same time, in America, we were redefining the family structure to include gay marriages and LBGTQ families. Of all of the strong career-women in my family that I introduced to the KOY, many saw the respect and appreciation for the women in the various family structures within the community.

For me, in my heart, I knew that I found a place that I thought personified the vision of what I desired the world to look like. Nothing I had witnessed before it seemed close. I finally could turn the chapter on my life pain and begin to work and love again with a new purpose: promote peace and health in the building of a new world.

7

What a Prestigious World We Created

Our language tricks us to believe white superiority
When I stayed with the KOY in October 2006, Hollywood released the film *The Prestige*, a new Hollywood movie about a magic show. For the life of us, we could not figure out why producers chose that title. *What does magic have to do with prestige?* Baffled, one of the leaders of the community looked up the Webster definition of prestige. To our surprise, it not only meant being held in high regard, it meant esteem based on the **perception** of one's achievements.

    We found this instantly eye-opening. *Prestige does not equate to absolute value or inherent importance.* In fact, what is deemed worthy of admiration is actually based on the perception of what is valuable. Stuck on this concept of perception, they did a bit of digging and found that the Latin and French origin of the word *prestige* is an illusion or a conjuring trick. We naturally then deduced that if colonizers mainly controlled the perception of what is important in our global society, then prestige was indeed a magical concept, rooted in trickery and lies.

    As of 2020, the Webster Dictionary still defines prestige as "widespread respect and admiration felt for someone or something on the basis of a **perception** of their achievements or quality." Realizing this only confirmed something that the KOY teaches all of its members: that the English language is fraught with deception. As such, the KOY teaches all of its children Hebrew as their first language.

As for the rest of us, we too need to confront the limits of English and redefine how we talk in this world. Because in the context of global white supremacy, it is clear that English is indeed a weapon of control and domination through trickery. And thus, what we hold as prestigious is nothing more than the result of a massive magic show. The high cost of a ticket to this show is internalized arrogance and racism.

Language defines our reality

So, am I taking the English language too seriously? Isn't it a tool to be used at an individual's discretion? Well, at the risk of being too critical, I'd argue that how we define and wield the English language is at the root of our racism. The deception embedded in our language allows us to bend it toward our bias. And in the end, English continues to assign superiority to whiteness. When we look at a magic show the trickery does not happen in plain sight, there is a distraction causing an illusion of sorts and the trickery happens where we cannot see. Applying this to our white culture, it is not only what we are taught that tricks us, it is what we are not taught that makes it the most harmful.

For example, in American schools, the concept of history is our greatest weapon of prestige. Throughout our education we are rarely taught about other cultures. We are only taught about American history until the tenth grade. This subconsciously creates a culture of ignorance because we know very little about cultures other than our own. Therefore, we cannot make value judgments about their traditions or about how they interact with others because we know nothing about them.

We do not get to compare and contrast our approach to anyone else's to measure the results of our decisions. We *do* learn that many of them strive to come here to the US. We *do* learn about *our* culture. The question is why? We cannot accept this as circumstantial or accidental. This was intentional to create an arrogant and ignorant population of what other cultures bring to the planet.

The deception does not end there. Our concept of history is riddled with misnomers that do not reflect the contributions of people of color. Arrogantly, we call European history "World History." Yet and still, our focus on Europe fails to tell even half the story. While we learn about the various insurrections that altered Europe, we never see how starting in the 13th century, the black Moors of Africa played the most significant role in building the infrastructure of European nations. Why don't we learn about the connection between this and American slavery?

Calling myopic European history "World History" is by design, and by design, it harms us by not telling the truth. One of the most hurtful consequences of the lies is that they render white and melanated children intellectually helpless. White children walk off with a deadly sense of superiority while children of color feel as if the only way to win is to aspire to whiteness.

The language then allows us to view wars being won as a part of our American greatness. Many of us began or begin each school day reciting "The Pledge of Allegiance to the Flag" without questioning why. We pledged our allegiance while failing to appreciate the black lives that built the country for said flag. We opened our sporting events singing the national anthem, thereby equating sport with war. In addition, we were taught that America is "the greatest nation on earth." And while our military fights for "*our* freedom," our schools never question why all of the battles took place on foreign land.

Indoctrinated, we low-melanated children were tricked into premature and unearned arrogance based on the moral acceptance of slavery, war and conquest. I remember being taught in World History at Saint Louis University that the Christians were right in the eyes of God because we won the wars. And that's why many whites falsely believe that the only culture worthy of making decisions about the governance of the world looks white and speaks English.

Even those of us who recognize this problem have trouble understanding the depth of the subconscious effect. This makes us want to be the ones who solve the issues, often not recognizing that we still have not learned another way to make decisions. We use the same learned values and characteristics hoping for different results rather than being able to value other cultures enough to learn from them.

Only recently has the magic show begun dimming its glitzy lights enough to reveal the value of other cultures, their accomplishments and their life-affirming relationship to the planet. But with progress comes threats to change. The Common Core education policy passed nationally has granted journalists, rather than scholars and historians, the power to write our children's precious curriculum. At the same time, new efforts have mounted to erase slavery from the school history books.

QUESTION: What is the magic show distracting us from? America's neo-colonization of Africa? The degradation of our environment? The poisoning of our children with violent media and disease-causing food? How about the greatness of other cultural practices and their relationship to the planet that provides us all with life?

Words have power, let's examine them! Another great example of the trickery inherent in the English language are the words ***spelling, cursive, translation,*** and ***conversation*** that describe how we document and communicate. One of the first things I learned when meeting the KOY leadership is that all of these terms have some tie-in to control and illusion. ***Spelling*** because we are under a spell, ***cursive*** because we are under a curse (even though learning cursive is better for brain development) (Askvik, Van der Weel, & Van der Meer, 2020), ***translate*** because we are in a trance, and we use ***con*** as a prefix in so many words and the word itself means to trick. Doesn't this seem odd to you that these are the names that are given for these words?

The ever-so-powerful word ***media*** is also a tricky one. It derives from the concept of medium which is a vehicle that transports ideas. But "medium" has a spiritual connotation as it also describes a person that can tune into your spiritual frequency. It's no wonder why the ***media*** has become so effective in racking up our fears and overriding our intuition with non-stop information.

The power to define

Ben Ammi's book, *God, The Black Man and Truth (GBT)*, drove home for me how our language has helped keep Americans in our racist state of mind. The second chapter "Power to Define" had the greatest impact on my understanding of what we are up against in this battle for changing the mindset that governs us. Ben Ammi wrote that "The Power to Define is the power to direct minds and conditions that will cause specific results in a [political] struggle... In fact, the Power to Define is one of the greatest weapons ... used to control [humans] and nations."

Take for example the concept of "freedom" during the Civil Rights Movement of the 1960s, Ben Ammi explained. The powers-to-be made sure the term freedom meant assimilation into the current white culture of America. But assimilation was not the goal of more "militant" groups such as the Black Panthers and The Nation of Islam. The freedom these groups sought required establishing their own culture on their own land or attaining equitable access to resources. This all hinged on achieving the same legal rights and protections as white Americans. Needless to say, the white establishment didn't approve of this definition of freedom for blacks, even though it is the definition we would use for our own selves.

Still today, there is a glaring difference between the freedom many blacks want and the freedom white legislators and police grant black humans. Every year we celebrate Dr. Martin Luther King Jr.'s dream. Yet before he was assassinated, he admitted that his dream of integrating blacks and whites was indeed walking his people into a "burning building." We white people need to be careful with this notion of freedom. We must step back and let black people define it for themselves. There is this fantasy that blacks want to assimilate into whiteness. And that by simply sharing space, we afford black people freedom. That simply is not the case in many instances. Rather freedom is the power to define and create your reality - by yourself and within your realm of culture, spirituality and beliefs.

Suppressing black's freedom

Often, white people's power to define is used to create a diversion from the issue of repairing our deeply rooted racism. One of the best examples of this is the conservative white response to NFL quarterback Colin Kaepernick's protest on the football field. In August of 2016, Kaepernick, a biracial black Italian, began a peaceful protest to bring awareness to the police brutality and killings of black people and the inequities that need repair.

Instead of standing for the national anthem, he would simply kneel on the grass. Game after game, Kaepernick kneeled, especially as the justice system failed to bring any of the cops to justice. He was so effective in his statement that other players joined him until the NFL could finally no longer stay silent. Facing jeers and leers from the audience, they continued to evoke their freedom of speech to try and put a stop to the brutality.

Yet the most popular person on TV at the time, President Donald Trump, began to say that these NFL players, especially Kaepernick, hated the country and disrespected the military and the flag of the USA. Suddenly, the issue of systematic racism got lost in the question of patriotism. Trump and other conservatives used their power to define and to create the illusion of a greater moral crisis to undermine the protests. By defining the protests as a question of patriotism and not freedom of speech, they were able to claim the higher ground and neglect their responsibility to do something about racism.

This backfired on Trump big time on January 6, 2021, when hundreds of rioters, almost exclusively white, stormed the U.S. capitol in one of the worst displays of white angst in hundreds of years. Five people were killed and yet the police managed to arrest zero people that day. This sparked the world to once again witness the miracle of white privilege as everyone knew that had those rioters been black, they wouldn't have lived to see another president sworn into office. This stunning irony led a white Yale Professor of History, Timothy Snyder, to aptly Tweet, "When black people and their allies exercise freedom of speech it's called violent insurrection. When white racists carry out violent insurrection it's called freedom of speech."

I would add that when black humans are justifiably hurt and angry, we define it as dangerous and hateful of our country and when white people act out their hate in murderous destructive ways we find ways to justify the acts based on their pain and anger.

What's in a name?

Have we ever stopped to ask ourselves why major U.S. metropolitan cities boast areas dedicated to the name of Asian and European ethnic groups? Little Tokyo, Chinatown, Little Armenia, and Koreatown, are just a few examples. Yet, we don't allow the labeling of areas that have a mostly black population to demonstrate the pride of that area. In St. Louis City, which has a majority black population, a street proudly called Barack Obama Avenue was reduced from a miles-long stretch to a mere block named after our first black man who served as president. Are we so fearful of black power and autonomy that we don't allow blacks to call their towns Blacktown or whatever name they choose to identify and connect with? Are we unwilling to allow blacks their own neighborhood names because we then have to concede that they are redlined by race and underfunded on purpose, as well as targeted for the sale of drugs, alcohol and firearms?

Alas, in Oklahoma, when a "black town" finally named itself Black Wall Street, what did whites do? A few years later, the government came in and completely bombed and destroyed the town. Because when left to be, black towns can consolidate and flourish. And once blacks flourish, white insecurity retaliates with violence. Our fear of black strength comes out as hate. Sadly now, rather than bombing black towns, our society has gotten too good at killing black dreams before they can grow.

8

My Growth in the Kingdom of Yah

A white leader in a black organization
Not long after my trip to Israel, I returned to LA to reflect on my life. I tried venturing back into the music industry but the up-and-coming artists under my management couldn't capture the time and investment of bigger agents. I realized that my connections were better suited for those who were at the top of the game. I was not as useful for artists in the beginning stages of building a career. Facing these roadblocks, I had no choice but to reinvent myself. After nights of worrying, I followed my instinct to be more involved with The Kingdom of Yah. Being a white man in an all-black organization might cause others to distrust me I fretted. But as time went on and music industry doors closed, my passion for a new venture overrode any fears.

My lifeline came in August of 2005 when Amikham, flew to LA to formally introduce me to influential leaders in the KOY. Sar Amiel, the leader of its emerging LA extension and I shared a vision for a peaceful, business-powered community and this sparked an immediate camaraderie. Sar, a tall, charming and focused man in his late 50s, soon invited me to live with him and many others in their shared home. As we started to expand the new LA community and its flagship restaurant, I stepped up to leverage and expand our signature Ginger Surprise drink and other products such as our packaged salads and vegan mac-and-cheese.

Not leaving music behind totally, I also volunteered to help market Shadayah's new musical album, which Sar Amiel produced in their in-house studio. However, the more I got involved, the more internal problems I realized I brought to the process as a white man. As I did with Nelly, I caught another bad case of the white savior syndrome.

Although I believed deeply in the mission of the KOY, having the answers satisfied something within my ego that I still struggle with today. Without taking the time to build relationships and trust, any value that I am able to bring may not be received. Six years of involvement and many broken bonds later, I realized how much this leadership error blindsided my passion and ambition. In the end, I not only lost precious friendships, but I also squandered thousands of investment dollars and wound up living with personal debt and regret.

To truly help my fellow white people understand how to recognize this white-savior syndrome and better lead in non-white spaces, this leg of my story is worth telling in detail.

Differences brought forth mixed emotions

In January of 2006, I left my one-bedroom apartment in the South Bay of LA to move into a five-bedroom house in Eagle Rock with Sar, eight other adults and seven children ages 1 to 11. The two-story home afforded me a plot in the living room with some of the other brothers. Though tiny, that space was the center of my massive life experiment in communal living that the KOY prides itself on.

Never had I experienced living with so many people. Still, I grew to love it. My social needs were constantly met by my fellow brothers, while the women - working on rotating shifts - guaranteed three fresh vegan meals a day to every member of the house. Together, we shared everything: a car, cell phones, laptops, money, and definitely household chores. To nourish our minds and beliefs, we attended weekly Friday classes. Sometimes during the classes, we reinterpreted biblical writings, and during others we analyzed current news reportings or studied books such as *Power vs. Force, Inconvenient Truth,* and other current economic and political books.

When an issue came up, we resolved it one-on-one or the leaders would step in and moderate, deciding how to resolve it in a way that brought us together. Daily, we talked about business and the needs for the house. We prayed individually and as a group and made ourselves available for each other's emotional needs at any given moment. I was not used to praying so I found my own way to learn about my connection with the Creator by finding comfort in our group mission and daily interactions.

Being white, single, and not officially converted into the tribe, I was initially asked often about how I was doing. I embraced it as it made me feel a part of something special. Being different is also one of the reasons I rose to leadership, I believe. I offered a refreshing perspective, ample availability, and the ability to build trust by remaining humble and willing to learn.

Once assigned leadership within KOY, however, I struggled internally. Going from being a free-willing business agent to having others call the shots was not easy. Coming from this world where I had so much privilege and freedom to move around as I wanted, I was not ready to swallow my pride to follow such a strict regimen. As much as I appreciated the communal, shared-economy lifestyle, the success of it hinged on a strict code of discipline, bordering on military-like regulation, which I found limiting.

Like all KOY extensions across the world, the LA community consisted of ministers such as Sar, Crown Brothers, and sub-leaders such as me and Sar's wife who led the adult brothers and sisters. We all played key specific domestic and business roles. Together, we all answered to Ben Ammi, the founder of the KOY in Israel, who we called 'Father.' In fact, no key decisions made in the LA chapter could stand without Ben Ammi's approval and so this left me in a precarious position as an outspoken businessman who wanted to see things happen almost overnight. When it came to business, my following the strict instructions of the ministers smacked against my mentality of having bright ideas and others following my lead. "Get in on the ground level," Sar warned, "and show us you're willing to do the grunt work." "Okay, okay," I grumbled.

You can imagine the tension that started to build. There I was with my white self, finance degree and Nelly business experience in tow, wanting to make waves in a community that primarily desired to live together, support one another, and give up the ways of the crazy capitalist world. While I preached on growth strategies, they were much more concerned with the early stages of developing a new society, which meant a dogged focus on adhering to their founding principles and meeting their needs sustainably.

I struggled because I wanted to provide broad leadership and direction, but instead, I was required to do the small things such as setting up tables and tents at the farmers market where we sold our products, transporting food back and forth, and stocking shelves at affiliate stores. I understood I needed to prove myself and show that I'm a hard worker, but the desire to do more created an internal struggle. I felt my talents would have been better used elsewhere.

While I don't shy away from the grunt work, I'd rather focus on helping create strategies and larger business. Still, the need to save the day as the white guy with the knowledge and experience made me want to be a definitive change-maker in the LA extension of the KOY. While my knowledge and experience may have benefitted the extension, my approach was not aligned with the overall mission.

Throughout my time with the LA extension of the KOY, Sar Amiel and I had an up and down relationship. We sometimes disagreed on business decisions and behaviors of leadership. This grew to be a strain towards the latter years. In the beginning though, we shared many laughs and enjoyed listening to music together. We shared deep conversation about community building and the psychological and intentional strategies that go along with it. I greatly appreciate what I learned in those conversations.

'Money is not what drives us'

My savior mentality initially affected how I viewed our approach to the business. I went in thinking money alone and focusing on profit could solve a lot of our problems. But in August of 2005, I learned my first hard lesson that this capitalistic view wouldn't take me far in the KOY. During my second trip to Israel, Sar invited me to discuss the promotion of Shadayah's album with Ben Ammi. My first chance to talk with Ben Ammi, Tracee (my girlfriend at the time), Amikham, and my sister Khaya (formerly Jenny) who had been living in Dimona with the KOY for several months, joined me.

On our big day, we met with Ben Ammi, the legendary pioneer in his 60s with the youthful, bronze face of an ancient pharaoh, and the KOY International Ambassador, Nasik Asiel. Excited and nervous, I rehearsed what I'd say in this special gathering, being sure to explain our plans for Shadayah's album and my commitment to the vision. In my mind, I imagined Ben Ammi would be impressed by my speech and show gratitude.

We sat at a table and took turns speaking briefly to the leader. Tracee went first, then Khaya, and the Ambassador. Ben Ammi listened with rapt attention, nodding and smiling. Amikham then spoke about his love of Shadayah's album, even saying "Jesse has been such a great help. He brings so much zeal to the KOY and keeps introducing people to the community." Sar added that "Jesse's contributions to the LA extension have been immense. We look forward to working with Jesse, and other artists in the KOY."

I smiled ear to ear, humbled and still quite zealous. Suddenly, it was my turn to speak. I gathered my inner courage and began, "Thank you and Shalom father...." I had so much to say and didn't know where to start. "Last time I was here, I loved my experience so much. I saw such great value in The Kingdom, with its restaurants and music. I want to help in any way I can to turn that value into positive cash flow..."

Before I could finish my sentence, Ben Ammi abruptly interjected, ending my brief and unimpressive introduction. "Money is not what drives us," he said. "It's about the spirit." I agreed with him and wanted badly to finish my speech to show him that I get it, but Ben Ammi went on, overriding the moment. "You see in the Kingdom, we define love differently. A man can be an alcoholic who smokes, and his wife could buy him a bottle of cognac and a box of cigarettes for his birthday and say, 'baby I love you.' That is not how we want to define Kingdom love. We want to do the right thing to and for each other." *I am not only about money either, I just see it as a vehicle to accomplish some of our goals,* I thought. But the opportunity to verbalize this was gone.

Disappointed in myself, I turned red and managed to keep my composure. My first encounter with our leader did not go as planned. Ben Ammi then turned to Sar. "I heard the album and love the messages. I want our musicians of Israel to create the Kingdom sounds to go with those beautiful words." Sar nodded in obedience. "Thank you for coming," Ben Ammi said. We thanked him and walked out. "Why didn't you tell the story of how you felt when you saw that Ben Ammi had beat you to creating a world such as the KOY?" Sar asked me outside. We laughed about it and, in my heart, I felt regret for coming off as money-focused.

Over the next couple of years, I did redeem myself. I revisited Israel several times and on my fourth visit, I met with Sar and Ben Ammi again to discuss the promotional tour for Shadayah. This time with Nasik Emmanuel. Later that night, Ben Ammi gave me my Hebrew name "Yishai" which he said meant "spiritual wealth, a gift to my people." Since then, I was truly humbled and motivated to live up to such a title.

My fear of failure haunted me

Two years later, at the peak of the LA extension, about 20 adults and 14 children lived in two five-bedroom homes. Tracee and I had birthed a beautiful baby girl, Sydnee, in 2007. I instantly felt feelings I had never felt before now as a new dad. Sadly, Tracee and I had been off and on, struggling to make our relationship work. For months, we couldn't agree on our direction going forward and split indefinitely.

I agreed to let Tracee take Sydnee to visit Tracee's family on the east coast for a few months. In a twist of fate, her trip turned into a permanent move, with us agreeing for me to see my daughter frequently. It wasn't my ideal arrangement, but I figured I'd let Tracee take charge in defining the best solution for Sydnee. I did not want the court system to determine how my daughter was raised.

Back with KOY, the community and I worked long hours creating food, delivering it to the distributors, promoting products in local grocery stores, and running our small restaurant. We had a lot to brag about but the stress of maintaining the operation wore on us all. Little did I know that my eagerness to turn a profit on behalf of the cause would later clash in dramatic ways. As a business, we met constant struggle with our products in Whole Foods due to constant changes in FDA regulations. After the financial crash of 2008, it became clear that KOY LA could not advance without some serious cash investment. When it came to fixing these issues, my background in finance and family economic class proved useful, or so I thought.

In actuality, a fear of failure drove me, preventing me from planning clearly. I hopped on the phone with my sister and convinced her to put up some funds. My sister then called my mom and I reached out to Bubby. Altogether, they wired me $40,000 in capital. In hindsight, my attempt to save the day was very short-sighted. In the KOY, when money was needed, we tried to go and get it. Leadership then got to decide on where it went. Although Sar and I had every desire to scale up the business and pay back that investment, it became clear that the money wouldn't reap a profit that easily. Rather, the funds would go to covering living expenses and a few business enhancements.

The traditional investment model of utilizing funds to turn over rapid profit was simply not there. As time went by, I grew concerned that I would not be able to pay my family back any time soon. Sar also brought in an investment of $30,000 from a friend. Still, the money ended up getting absorbed across the community and business needs rather than being invested in a way that would translate to sustained revenue growth. Giving such a large sum of money appeased the white savior in me that really wanted to be a major contributing part to the solution. Sadly, it left my family in the lurch, not sure when I'd make good on their investment.

Trying to save face

About a month after putting up the money, I tried to call the shots on what we needed to do with Ginger Surprise and other products. I stopped to talk with our accounting person. She said, "Look, Jesse, there's only $3,000 left." Her words drew sharp claws across my scalp. Angered and baffled, I told her we could have gotten so much more money in the long run had we invested it in the business first and prioritized building credit. But there was nothing she or I could do. Within a month, we lost the lease on our first restaurant. Mulling over the loss of opportunity, I flung myself into running different aspects of the business and grew increasingly withdrawn.

A year and a half later, we opened our second restaurant with funds from work we did for a non-profit. But the funds came at a cost. At the non-profit's BBQ and health fair in Inglewood, I passed out the morning of the event too exhausted to participate in the setup after staying up all night to make the food. That was not a good omen for how the new restaurant would be run. Months went by, and even with success in reach, funds tightened to the point of causing several other members to leave the LA extension. This left Sar's brother Hosea and I to manage the brunt of the daily tasks, from cooking, packaging and distributing food, to marketing and sales.

Seven days a week, the work inundated us. While we hired much-needed help from outside of the community, we couldn't keep anybody on very long due to constant setbacks. It got so bad, I asked my friend DJ Sirrlos in St. Louis to fly in and help us out. A week after he arrived, Whole Foods slapped us with new FDA regulations, requiring us to remove our products from the shelves until they were met. To gain re-entry, we'd have to go through a third-party quality standards company. The strain brought out my workaholism and Sar's mean streak. One day, Sar brought a group of white folks to the restaurant to introduce them to the Kingdom. I joked and said that "they keep me locked in a room and only let me out to work." But Sar didn't find that funny. "Do you know how that looks?" he asked in disgust.

While trying to complete this new process, we fell behind on our restaurant rent again and lost the lease on the second location. Sirrlos continued to work without pay yet tensions sparked between Sar and me. To Sar, Sirrlos was living with us rent-free and Sar became increasingly resentful that he wasn't making cash contributions despite Sirrlos working for us day and night. Naturally, I pushed back against Sar leading to more tensions.

Our food business and Farmer's Market booth continued to be a silver lining. Every weekend, we sold hot vegan plates to dozens of customers. We also continued to drop off food to various stores around LA. Down to just Hosea and me, I cooked all of the food from our famous vegan breakfast sandwich to vegan kale greens, mac and cheese, vegetable lasagna, pot roast, black-eyed peas, cornbread and barbeque tofu. Our food had gotten so good, one man cried inside of an affiliate store when he found out they were out of our vegan breakfast sandwich, which one LA blogger described as "vegan crack." As fate would have it, one particular Saturday at the Farmer's Market shifted my life.

Hosea brought me over to a beautiful woman named Chevela who was helping another woman sell her vegan cobblers a few booths down from ours. Despite wearing a big puffy winter coat and hat, her sparkling smile and gorgeous braided black hair grabbed my attention. When Hosea told me she needed work, I lit up with both relief and intrigue. Not long after our first meeting, Chevela sat in the passenger seat of our delivery van, helping me drop products off at 10 stores. What fascinated me the most was how we talked effortlessly the entire time. Both giving people who felt our role in life was to help others, we had so much in common. Both parents, we bonded over life struggles which we shared with striking realness and a determination to overcome.

To my surprise, at the end of our grueling day, I said, "I like you, I like you. I haven't had a conversation like this in a long time…". She agreed then put her bare-naked feet in my lap and commanded "My feet hurt, rub these. You have worked me so hard." Not being a feet person, I was turned off instantly, yet I commenced to grab her feet. In my mind, knowing very well if I did, this had better become a long-term relationship. After that night, we continued seeing each other when time permitted and grew closer. Every time we got together, we had a running joke about how light-skinned she was despite being black. "You are whiter than me!" I'd say. As the stress mounted with the KOY, Chevela offered a breath of fresh air. Not to mention, Chevela had Beyonce curves and a personality that kept me on my toes.

More money problems

Scrambling still to save the day, I found two other investors that agreed to give $10,000 and $15,000 respectively. With the $10K, we signed a lease on a third restaurant location and were on our way to move back into Whole Foods. Sar and my relationship ebbed and flowed between camaraderie and frustration. The next day, the person who promised the $15K phoned and said he was on the way to the bank, only for me to realize that he'd never come through. This crisis caused just enough shock to rock Sar's trust in me. Despite getting a new restaurant, we now lacked the money to stock it. Loyalty being my most cherished value, I kept at the mission still, believing truly that we could make it work.

In 2011, after several years of wins and losses, I sought relationships with other vendors in Whole Foods who were also struggling to stay on the shelves. We discussed how we could leverage our resources in a supportive way to get back and stay in the Whole Foods operations. One of them was an Armenian man named Rodrique with a Middle Eastern food company. We formed a partnership.

After several attempts, I was introduced to an investor, another Armenian restaurant owner, who ended up knowing people in Rodrique's circle. However, as we moved on this, Sar reverted to his old suit and requested some of that investment capital upfront to pay bills. I resisted bringing this request to Rodrique as this was our last chance to survive and I didn't want to put the cart before the horse. Rodrique agreed to small advances from time to time but it was never enough.

Sar urged me to pressure Rodrique for more. I fought back in an attempt to think long-term and protect the new relationship.

Finally, we hit our lowest point. DJ Sirrlos, Chevela and I were inside the Rodrique's packaging facility when Sar called me to the parking lot to discuss the business. "I need you to get more money for our bills from Rodrique. We will pay him from future sales," he said. I flat out said, "Look, I got what I could and Rodrique said 'No.'" The tension grew until I said "F*ck this!" and walked back into the facility to continue working.

Sar came charging after me. Sensing danger, Chevela lunged in between us, placing her body in the middle of us. Sirrlos hung in the wing, waiting to see if Sar was going to make another move. Rodrique ended up yelling for us all to shut up and let Sar know that he was cash strapped and could not do anything until new money came in. Sar drove off, and I continued packaging the food, trying to shake off the heat of the altercation.

This last feud with Sar marked the beginning of the end of my time with the KOY in LA As hard as I tried, I couldn't submit to Sar's will and found his personality increasingly off-putting. Even worse, the investor with whom Rodrique and I made a deal was now being sued and could not fulfill anything close to his obligation. Soon after, I moved out of the KOY house and into an apartment owned by the investor.

Chevela, her son Stephen, and DJ Sirrlos moved in with me. Eventually, some money did come in and we were able to get back into Whole Foods. But Rodrique refused to pay Sar the amount he promised for licensing the KOY food items and brand we had developed. Rodrique inadvertently left me out of major decisions and once again, underfunding made us all grasp for what we had in our power to control.

By then, Sar had cut his losses with the LA extension and pledged to move to Chicago. The last blow to our bond came when he turned over the businesses to a new friend of his, rather than Hosea and me. With no money and no business, I had a lot of soul searching to do. As painful as it was, I had to face the limits of my power. I spent many nights angry and hurt over coulda, woulda, shoulda's until I woke up and faced the defeat.

Learning to lead differently

I had a lot of time to reflect on my experience. I cherished the opportunity to be a part of the community and value the mission at hand. I am still very much connected to and supportive of those still involved in fulfilling that mission. I appreciate the valuable lessons I received and the beauty of what I witnessed and experienced. I am still a brother to those with whom I worked and shared space during my journey.

To this day, I don't hold anyone responsible for what led to my choice to modify my relationship with the community. In scrutinizing my role in the events that took place, I see the error of my ways and the need to heal from my arrogance. Ultimately, when it comes to white people attempting to lead with or on behalf of black people, the danger of the white savior syndrome is ever-present.

This does not mean that white people should not try to invest in or help lead initiatives to ensure the liberation of black people in our society. Rather, we whites must beware of the pitfalls of the savior syndrome and choose instead to lead in a more conscious and supportive way, building trust and strong relationships in our efforts. We must also realize that the impact we can have as individuals is limited without the support of systemic correction. We must not let fear of mistakes and failure stop us. We must allow for feedback as hurtful as it may seem at times. It is all a part of our healing process.

Hope after the KOY

Just before we left Sar's family's house, Chevela's recently turned 7-year-old son Stephen sat me down and interviewed me. "So, what are your intentions? Do you like my mom? Soooo, she wants somebody who is, how do I say this? Responsible." He paused, thought for a moment, and then with a smile and serious tone he said, "And you need to buy me some gifts." With that crucial information, Chevela and I set out to support one another and overcome the past.

Six months into living together, Chevela and I had made it official. I'll never forget the day I saw her walking out of the apartment we just moved into. I felt that I was met with the promise of a new life. Now a father to two children, I knew I needed to make an adjustment to chart my path differently. Not only did I need to work on myself, I desperately needed to guide them through the world we live in, making sure that my black children had every opportunity to live up to their full potential.

9

Becoming a Father to Black Children

After the KOY, Chevela and I bounced from one area of LA to another for several years. We spent two years in Encino, which is located in the Valley of LA County. About six months into our relationship, on the way to dropping him off at school, Stephen asked me if I would be his dad. "Will you be my father," the 7-year-old asked sincerely. I knew his request was not something to be taken lightly. Chevela had already told me that at the age of 3, Stephen asked her when she was going to find him a father. He's always been a bright, loving and articulate boy. That day in the car, I didn't hesitate and said "Of course, I will."

I desired to raise a child and Stephen, with his great sense of humor, and I bonded naturally. At the start of our relationship, we'd tell jokes non-stop and make up songs that would parody life. We'd take the 'Twelve Days of Christmas' and turn it into the 'The twelve days after being caught cheating' or 'The twelve days of being bullied.'

My only concern was that Stephen's use of vernacular already exceeded my comprehension. He read at such a high level that his use of the English language was far superior to mine. I felt like I was talking to my father at times just trying to use the context of the word in the conversation to guess the meaning. Chevela and I loved his conversations with my dad over the phone. All my life, I joked with Larry to talk to me in short, six-letter words rather than his "Ivy League" language. That Stephen shared Larry's use of language made it easier to embrace the fact that we were truly related.

Having children has been one of the strongest reasons why I have committed myself to the transformation process. My relationship with Stephen, now a young black man, continues to remind me of the urgency of anti-racism. Spending many years in Inglewood and West Adams with its heavy policing and economic struggles, I witnessed firsthand how cops targeted black youth and how policies create an inopportune environment for its residents.

How can I help build the momentum of change? How can I help whites re-connect to the planet and humanity in a healthy way? This is what being an anti-racist is at its core. It is approaching each day with a love for living so that our actions intentionally improve the quality of life for all and inspire continuous creativity. In this setting, there is no mental or spiritual space for racism.

The great struggle led to greater empathy

Leaving the KOY and moving to the Valley at the age of 35 found me finally confronting my independence. This was complicated by the fact that both Chevela and I were financially broke at the time. Like never before, I had to build from the absolute bottom. I still had the privilege of getting some funds from family members, mainly my mom. But that support couldn't answer the overarching questions looming over my life. How do you raise a son and support a life partner and daughter with virtually nothing? How do you tackle all of life's demands when so many of the responsibilities seem to fall on you?

Despite being a young white man, I struggled to find 9-5 work that met the level of income needed to provide comfort. My resume suffered from a record of businesses that were no longer successful. I wasn't getting the interviews. I talked to entertainment management companies in hopes of using my talent to manage other artists. Yet in this world, you are only as valuable as your list of clients for which I had none at the time. After a while, it got to the point of "how am I going to pay the bills now?" Sitting down with Chevela, we'd go back and forth between a desire to invest in her line of skincare products and candles - and the ever-present promise of getting a conventional job.

CHEVELA Organics was a company she started during a stint of homelessness which left me enamored at her drive despite the odds. I wanted deeply to continue my entrepreneurial pursuits and looked to help sell her product and stock up inventory any chance I got. As days ticked by, it became clear that neither CHEVELA Organics nor my other interests would pay off overnight. The struggle was constant and some days we'd resort to counting coins in the car and celebrating when he had just enough to get Taco Bell.

How do you balance poverty with raising a son? All of Stephen's friends would go to game rooms or other family activities. How do I explain to my son that Dad doesn't have the funds to let him go, yet again? During the struggle, I got to experience humanity in a way that made me see just how hard it is living in America. One thing I realized is how expensive it is to be broke. For example, if I can't go to the grocery store and get everything I need for the week, I'll end up spending more in terms of gas and time by going every other day as money trickles in. It's the little inconveniences like these that add up to big costs.

There's also the personal danger that poverty puts people in. We began our relationship at Sar's house taking Stephen to school on the bus when we had no car. The first car that was ours was a crappy old 1990 Chrysler minivan Rodrique gave me so I could work with him during the last attempt to keep the food going. The shocks on the minivan were so bad that any bump would gyrate Chevela and my entire body. We began to flinch into bracing ourselves for the trauma in fear when we saw a dip in the road.

After things did not work with Rodrique, he took the car away when he saw me at an event at Whole Foods. I was working for our manufacturing partner to help reduce some of the debt Rodrique left us with when he refused to pay Sar or pay for any of A Taste of Life's portion of the business. He thought I turned on him, so he took the van. Go figure.

With no car once again, a close friend of mine, Sal, bought me one. It was a ten-year-old Chrysler Sebring that he purchased from someone he knew. He got it for such a great price we thought his friend must be looking out for him. A couple of days into riding it, we realized it had a terrible transmission. Putting our lives in danger, we'd have to shift the car into neutral on the highway because it couldn't get out of second gear until turning it off then on. Only then the car would find the proper gear to handle faster speeds.

Driving from Encino, Chevela and I would say to the car, "We love you. Please get us over the mountain and into LA so we can handle our business today. We know you can do it." Eventually, the car wouldn't do anything other than second gear, so we couldn't take the highway. We'd rev it up to 40 miles an hour then let it coast in neutral over and over again through the streets to our destinations.

Finally, after a year of cars that caused mental anguish, we were able to purchase our own used Ford minivan. After picking up the van, we whizzed around LA to downtown for Chevela to file a business matter and zipped back to Encino to pick up Stephen from school. In the car, we all celebrated that moment. It took us less than half the time to get around as it normally did.

Managing stress

Searching constantly to build stability and reach our personal goals mounted the stress. Chevela and I each needed time to work through our past individual issues as we began our new phase. With the present stressors adding so much to our plates, we did not have the time or space to heal, nor could we lean on each other for support. This led to constant fighting. Due to the financial woes, we also moved a lot, which caused Stephen to switch schools every year or two. After two years in the Valley, we moved to the southern part of Inglewood, a slice of LA called "The Bottom." At times it lived up to its name given its gang violence and poverty.

Months after moving in bullets came flying through the wall of the apartment bathroom. The owners of the building, an elderly black couple, ran such a slumlord operation with this building and others they owned. Our plumbing backed up and we could no longer use our kitchen sink and one of the showers. We had to fight to get out of the contract. While in Inglewood, I began substitute teaching and consulting for small businesses and we were able to get out to an area near where Chevela grew up called West Adams. The struggle continued as rental rates were growing through the roof, but we decided to lay some roots there with the hope of rebuilding our lives.

All while raising a son

Added to this struggle was the strain of raising a black boy into a man. Every time Stephen left the house, Chevela grew anxious in ways that I had not considered the severity of until I shared the role as a parent. We both tried to push Stephen to find as many activities as we could, but he was too young to understand and appreciate. We wanted to keep him out of harm's way and give him skills that he could use later. Yet, he was feeling overwhelmed. He just wanted to develop friendships and enjoy life as a child.

When Stephen hung with his black friends, his mother worried about how they would be received and treated by police, store managers, or other adults. For example, when he went to the mall with more than two friends, the mall cops asked them to separate because more than three black boys together were seen as a gang. We worried how the police or actual gang members would view them. When he hung with his white friends, Chevela worried what if they did normal boy activities that could get them in trouble. It would be easy for the white children to get away with mischief, especially because they could either voluntarily blame Stephen or be coerced into blaming him. In doing so, he would suffer the worst fate among them.

If Stephen traveled to a predominantly Latino community, she worried that gangs would see a handsome young black boy and want to cause him harm. Chevela had spent many years in gang intervention where it was known in those circles the impact of the government's Co-Intel Pro - that large mandate created by J Edgard Hoover to intentionally break down the black panther party and black communities. This mandate also required covert actions of the government to pit black and brown skinned communities against each other.

The constant vigilance required to safeguard the family against these threats led to internalized rage which often erupted at the oddest times. We'd find ourselves venting on a poor employee at Taco Bell, raising a muck simply because they charged us extra for substituting cheese for lettuce. "You're charging us for lettuce with no nutritional value! Really?"

"Uh, no ma'am. Sorry about that." They replied. We can laugh about that now, but at the time all of the combined stresses around money and Stephen made me better understand the emotional toll of just how hard it is to raise a family and survive racism in this country. To do so not only necessitates a daily heroic effort to make ends meet. It also demands a godly level of self-discipline to avoid self-destruction or harming others.

Getting my PsyD became my get-out-of poverty plan

In 2014 I called a friend, Mark from Indianapolis, who gave me an ingenious idea that would indeed bring some temporary relief. "Apply to school. It's the Ghetto Bank. You'll get the money you need!" he said. Alas, I researched graduate programs and found the Phillips Graduate Institute/University, which has since merged with Campbellsville University in California. Considering my experience in structuring and managing businesses, the organizational psychology PsyD interested me the most. I applied, got in, and attained a sizable student loan, enough to partially float Chevela and me for the next three years.

Throughout my first semester of my PsyD, I had to leave the house at 5 am and take three buses and a train to get to school by 8 am so that Chevela had access to the van. From time to time, my mom helped me financially and so I was able to catch up on late bills and pay for Stephen's clothes, gaming systems, and piano and acting lessons. Through my toughest days, I kept thinking about how getting this degree would help me boost my credentials and tap into a new network.

Along the way, the PsyD program taught me how systems are created and managed beginning with the values, vision, mission and goals of those who design them and manage them. The results are often realized much further down the line. Yet, because results are more tangible and are measurable, people often focus on trying to modify the results without addressing the root values and mission.

The ideas for transformation can seem simple but the implementation can be challenging because of the need to address the emotions, thoughts, and intentions that need to change to achieve different results. This process needs coordination, transparent communication, trust-building and commitment throughout. Then we must be willing to manage the ebbs and flows and work through conflict. Suppression and denial, as opposed to addressing the differences that lead to conflict, are the biggest threats to the effectiveness of the change process.

Given what I experienced in community building in the KOY and my lifelong journey to fight racism, what I learned in my PsyD program helped me better identify what shifts need to take place in our colonial world. We low-melanated folks needed to alter our approach. Some of the awareness of this need for change was already happening due to advances in technology and a less segregated society. Newer generations have a different outlook on managing economies.

For me, I could identify the problems that aboriginal and indigenous folks faced. Having lived through economic challenges and learning organizational psychology, I empathized even more with the emotional weight carried by the black and brown communities. We cannot continue to ignore the need for reparations. My new mission was set. Anti-racism needs to be a healing process.

The challenge is that the values of those in power have not changed. Therefore, those in power continue to shift as society shifts in order to maintain their power. Just like so many others who struggle financially, being able to focus on this new mission was a challenge I sought to overcome.

Talking to my children about race

My beautiful daughter Sydnee is very much loved by her mother (Tracee) and me. Although for me, our relationship is strained. We are separated due Tracee's move with her to the East Coast. Sydnee grew uneasy about developing a relationship with me separately. I now rely heavily on hopes and prayers that my relationship with my daughter will be fully revived. For the first ten years, I could still visit and see my daughter. During this time, I'd try to instill within her an awareness of her race and self-love.

When Sydnee was young, she had very light skin to the point of being mistaken by other whites for white when she went out with my mother. Black folks could tell she was "mixed race." Between these worlds, I'd sit down and teach her a bit about race. After swimming, one day when my mother and I shared duties of being with Sydnee in the pool, we both ended up skin burned While Syd got a beautiful tan.

I told her that her melanin is her superpower. I was very excited when she reminded me of what I taught her during my next visit four months later. Still, to this day, I want Sydnee to love herself and know that the ideas of Dr. Martin Luther King ring true about how we should judge a person. I also want her to be aware that racism is real and that it can impact relationships as she gets older. As for my son Stephen, his mother and I know the battle will be tough. When Stephen dates white girls, for example, we are concerned about how her family will react. We worry about how adults will react in public. The legacy of Emmitt Till, the young black boy brutally murdered by white passersby for whistling at a white woman in Money, Mississippi, in August of 1955, still lingers in America today.

Black boys are more likely to be set up by their white peers when things go wrong. If a white parent is embarrassed by the behaviors of their child, blaming the black kid is a far too acceptable response because whites are subtly programmed to believe that criminal type behavior is natural to black boys. When the police are searching for someone to pin something on, it's an easier conviction to pin it on the black child. They have been trained to coerce answers that fit their stories either by using scare tactics or through other forms of manipulation.

As for white children, they can be tricked or scared into cooperating without the intent to harm their black friends. They end up cooperating out of a need to save themselves. These racialized inclinations bring about a high level of concern for parents of black children that white parents do not even have to consider.

In 2020, Stephen grew old enough to get a state ID. On the day he went to apply, he wore a white T-Shirt. His mom and I ended up arguing with him about putting on a different type of shirt for the ID picture. We were concerned that if he had run-ins with the police, they'd choose to look at the T-Shirt as gang wear and associate him with the streets. Stephen felt like it was ridiculous that in 2020 he should not be allowed to wear a T-Shirt for his ID.

It is ridiculous. We agreed. Still, we had legitimate concerns that we would not have had if he were white. How police target black men goes back to the end of slavery. We just wanted to minimize his risks of injury. The argument escalated and Stephen walked off. Since then, he has been more willing to accept that we are simply trying to protect him, both physically and psychologically.

Chevela challenged me to talk to white people

Despite our struggles, Chevela and I talked about anything and everything. From her I learned to see the world differently. For example, and very ironically, Chevela felt anger toward successful black men who married non-black women. For one, Chevela taught me about the level of nurturing from a black mother. Being that black is the original skin color, we all can be traced back to having come from her. Black women throughout our history for sure have endured so much thrown their way and yet remained the foundation of their households and communities.

"Society ignores our power and when someone who came from a black woman shares their success with someone who is not, it hurts," she said. Not only that, but what happens in case the marriage dissolves or he dies, the transfer of wealth goes away from the black community once again. These may seem like "reverse-racism" concerns, but as I learned to understand where Chevela was coming from, I realized that criticizing this point of view is unfair to black women if it is done without correcting the system put in place to break up the black family and oppress these communities as a whole.

One area that Chevela helped me with the most was pushing me out of my comfort zone. I can have great conversations with just about anyone no matter what they look like, yet my comfort was being in black spaces and interacting with melanated people. She told me, "It is great that you know what you know, and you want to spend time with us and are so genuine in the way you show up. But if you really want to help, then you need to go talk to your people and get them to correct their ways." That was the hardest thing to hear. I have been told before to leave my friends alone and go with my people to use my privilege to get into doors that they could not. Make money and then come back. And at times I wish I could have had the political savvy to do so. It made me want to throw up to think about playing those games.

This was different though. Chevela wasn't telling me to play like someone I wasn't to get access to resources. She was asking me to be exactly who I am in white circles. Go there and share my perspective. Go there and open up eyes. Lead people to wanting to help out. At first, I whined and cried to myself. I did not want to. I talked with white folks in certain situations, and many were oblivious to the fact that racism still exists. The idea of a need for reparations was so far removed from their thought processes that I felt frustrated at the ignorance of my people. Some of that began to change with the murder of Mike Brown, Eric Gardner and others. The idea of police brutality being a problem started to sink in. Yet we were far from discussing what equity looks like, how horrible our past has been, and the nuances of how television programming is used to create a semblance of post-racist society.

The weaponization of segregation and gentrification still made for a growing wealth gap and police are used as part of a greater system to disrupt and discourage economic progress and community building. Are white people ready to grasp this? Discussing the media's portrayal of melanated humans vs. whites, or how the hiring process leads to homogeneity and that becomes a natural suppressor of those who do not fit the profile were concepts I'm sure most whites often misunderstand. Often these were the good-hearted white folks. They wanted to help if there was a problem. Nevertheless, many did not see the depth of the problem or have the understanding of how they showed up in spaces toward the humans that they wanted so badly to help.

Yet the challenge we face as low-melanated folks is that those who we're fighting for now that we do not struggle the same way they do on a daily basis. We often wanted a quick fix or to be appreciated for what we are doing. While that is a natural feeling for us, the humans we are helping are not responsible for those feelings.

We must extend ourselves beyond acknowledging that generations of our white folks before us have harmed the communities we are serving. We must recognize that we are still doing that today and that our approach to world domination has harmed and continues to harm the planet. Our practices that give us inequitable advantages make it difficult for us to have relationships with others and see their value. Truly accepting this takes humbling and before that, it takes a willingness to gain an understanding and acknowledge these truths for ourselves.

For me, following the direction that Chevela was giving me in taking on this mission was not something I felt equipped to do. The same challenge many white folks have with relating to humans of color on a deeper level of connection I faced reaching my own white people. And then came the Donald Trump presidency. Ah, thank goodness Toto pulled the curtain back and we could see that the wizard of our deception is not a beautiful utopia we call post-racial America. Not only do systemic racism and the devaluing of humans who have more melanin still exist, but there also exists a weaponized hate for these humans by those of us who lack that level of melanin.

Thankfully, Donald Trump blew past the republican candidates like a torch in a brushfire. His racism was authentic, engrained, and out on display for the rest of us to see, from his approach towards people of color who wanted to enter the country to the support of police and degradation of peaceful protestors of justice. My good-hearted democrats hated this type of overt racism so much that they could not see the racism in their candidates. Hilary Clinton, Bill Clinton, Joe Biden, and the rest of the bunch have helped put in place harmful, racist policies and avoided real reparative justice.

They may have been willing to share a little more of the pie in certain ways. They have paid greater attention to the cultural differences and can speak about the harm done with a greater level of appearing to care. But many of the followers just couldn't see they were not who they wanted us to believe that they were. Trump altered that and forced us to look at the true heart of America. As a result, Trump challenged progressive people like me to get our shit together. He, along with the extreme violence taking place in America, were enough to convince me that Chevela was right. My aim would be to get out there and work with as many white people as I can to move us toward reparative healing.

My goal now is clear. I must talk to whites about how to heal racism from within. At the same time, as a dad, I must share my experience with parents raising non-racist children as my parents raised me. My mom and dad went out of their way to show me the humanity of others and build within me a healthy distrust of the system which is steadily trying to break us apart. And that is something every child needs to understand before stepping out into this world.

10

The Struggle to Fit In

In 2016, I learned that white anti-racism organizations exist. It was the day after Trump was elected and I heard about the protests on a progressive free speech radio station KPFK. I knew of the multi-racial coalition Black Lives Matter, but I was surprised to hear about White People 4 Black Lives (WP4BL) in Los Angeles. I immediately thought, "Hey, that's me." I drove straight home, hopped on the internet and learned how I could participate. WP4BL is a collective of activists currently operating within a national network of white anti-racists called Showing Up for Racial Justice (SURJ). Rooted in dismantling white supremacy, WP4BL act in alliance with Black Lives Matter Los Angeles, the Movement 4 Black Lives, and other partners.

Not only did WP4BL have regular strategy meetings, but there was also a monthly discussion group that appealed to me. It was called the Alliance of White Anti-Racists Everywhere - LA (AWARE-LA) and appeared to provide a healthy outlet for processing the reality of racism through dialogue, the value of which I truly appreciate as long as it leads to actionable transformation. A couple of weeks after researching their organization, I attended my first discussion group in December and a WP4BL meeting the following week. Not sure how involved I wanted to be, I simply showed up hoping to move the needle forward.

Scratching the surface of racial justice

AWARE-LA meetings were in a small church room in Santa Monica. They were used to having meetings with about 15 people. Now, thanks to the Trump election, there were 60 people. Within a few months that grew to about 100 consistently. Before each meeting, all of the newbies had to read "Characteristics of White Supremacy Culture" an article by Kenneth Jones and Tema Okun. The first time I read the article, I felt empowered with a key tool to communicate the issues of our disconnected culture. I now had a clear explanation for my saying, "fuckin' white people," which is my kneejerk reaction to day-to-day observations of our culture of privilege and harm.

They spoke about the need for an all-white space to work through our shit without further burdening black folks to constantly have to teach us. We later split into groups to ask questions for anyone to respond to as an open dialogue. We each were allowed to come up with one question for the group. I remember having to control my zeal and not answer every question. I spent the first few meetings mainly observing who was who and at what level of understanding they were. After my first meetings with AWARE-LA and WP4BL respectively, I asked the leaders to meet with me so I can introduce myself and offer whatever support I could give to their mission.

Through the white anti-racism groups I met amazing people, including my mentor Bob Gordh, an articulate reparations advocate. They also engaged me with high-level, meaningful activism. However, many of the people joining the discussions were new to the ideas that racism still needed to be addressed. Therefore, much of the awareness and discussions exchanged were often surface level. Many participants were in touch with the obvious economic statistical disparities, the police murders, and whatever they had witnessed through the media and from exchanges with people of color at work.

Often members, other than the leadership who had been involved for years prior to Trump's election, didn't seem able to understand or weren't interested in diving into the 'why' racism exists or the outward practiced racist behaviors that were programed subconsciously. Structurally provided advantages for us white folk were acknowledged to a point, yet often were not seen as an issue of harm that we should address. To me, this proved to be one of the biggest hurdles to a more effective progressive strategy.

This was especially true for the Democratic Socialists of LA (DSA-LA) and other progressive groups who wanted to support BLM. Despite a strong mission of racial justice, race-focused solutions hadn't permeated DSA-LA subgroups focusing on the environment, health or housing. In turn, broad strategies relied on the good of social policy alone to autocorrect for racial disparity, rather than targeting racism at its root. People would say, well "healthcare for all helps all people," or "a clean environment helps all people."

As well-meaning as they were, many members of DSA-LA falsely hoped that by correcting other social issues, they would automatically address racism and uplift all people of color including black folks. In reality, countless researchers showing examples of missed opportunities such as FHA and VA support have disproved this approach. And that's why I vehemently opposed it. Race should have been the lens through which we addressed the other issues.

Fixing the other issues through racial justice will automatically fix them for all races and not the other way around.

I understand that progress is gradual. The basis of any lasting transformation hinges on providing equitable resources to all. Coinciding with these policies, however, is a burning need to address the disparity within the policy itself. We need to take into account how decisions are made, by whom, and the same for how the policy is implemented and enforced.

What many now realize is that we must strive for racial justice concurrently with other issues of social justice or risk perpetuating the racism that continues to harm so many. In tandem with healthcare-for-all for example, must be efforts to equalize the food industry that provides less than healthy options in abundance in black neighborhoods. We must also address the existing problems that block access for black entrepreneurs to grow, manufacture and scale healthy food products.

The same goes for housing. The quality of the housing must be equal, streets must be repaired, and homes and assets must be equitably valued. Access to quality local amenities such as parks, swimming pools and various sporting activities must also be addressed. It's not enough to make sure that everyone has a roof over their head. Addressing these housing issues also improves the environment and reduces stress, which improves health.

Most importantly is the ability for each community to manage these resources for themselves without our control. These and other important issues are all interwoven in our system. Without this clear racial justice lens, many whites are quick to propose noble actions that lack the strength of a true commitment to black lives. Even after making the decisions, implementing the changes are challenging due to built in racism.

Take for example a current situation, the aid to farmer's that was built into the Covid-19 relief bill that was the Biden administration's first large achievement. According to The New York Times article by Alan Rappeport on February 21, 2022, almost nine months after it was signed, black farmers are facing the possibilities of losing their business. They are still waiting on the fund promised to keep them afloat.

White farmers are claiming discrimination about funds allocated to repair years of proven discrimination and the courts are holding the funds. Meanwhile, other government agencies and banks are looking to foreclose on the black business who made decisions based on these promises. White folks get the advantage going in and are allowed the power to stop the repair. And as time goes on, the amount needed to repair the situation grows.

It was hard to find my place amongst my people

Upon learning of AWARE-LA I also immediately joined the Jewish antiracism group, which was started by Jewish members of WP4BL. Here, I encountered similar challenges fitting in. Here I was with my fellow Jews, but I felt so different. I went to an early-stage planning meeting and proposed the idea that to be the most effective, we should be willing to acknowledge that our white ancestors are not the direct lineage of the black and brown Hebrew-speaking Israelites. In fact, we are the direct descendants of the Greco-Roman and Caucasian Jews who traveled to Africa and the Middle East to learn and steal from the Egyptians and Israelites. I was ignored. I didn't mind because, to me, I was planting a seed and observing the responses.

With WP4BL, AWARE-LA, and in later years, discussion groups in St. Louis, (AROC and Witnessing Whiteness), I pushed to keep the truth of history and what our true intentions were in focus. I wanted to support the organizations as a whole without taking over the show. I felt my best contribution would be in educating others and demonstrating how I interacted and showed my solidarity with melanated humans.

In the process, I attempted to join some of the subgroups as well. In WP4BL, I participated in an offshoot that led the facilitation of new member orientation. After the first meeting, I became a distraction because I was too busy teaching about the issues such as Co-Intel Pro than focusing on how the organization worked. I couldn't help myself and soon agreed that the subgroup wasn't right for me.

I surprisingly struggled also with fitting into the team that led the teaching part of the monthly meetings. I enjoyed my time and interactions with folks, but when I disagreed with them about a particular topic during my first planning meeting, I found myself in conflict resolution. There were quite a few Jews involved in WP4BL. With the rise of white nationalist groups, it suggested that we teach how these groups were using anti-Semitism to attract new members.

I voiced my opposition to focusing on this as it would take our focus off of black lives. The matter ended up in a conflict resolution session. It was a process where two members facilitated a discussion between those who brought up the conflict and me. There were also observers involved who were to remain available for reflection if needed. The goal was to find a resolution to the conflict and define how to move forward. This was followed by a more open and receptive discussion with the same subgroup facilitators.

I learned a lot from this conflict resolution process. The groups of Jews who asked for the meeting opened up about the importance of the Jewish teachings to their approach to racial justice. They also thanked me for keeping us focused on working for the justice of black folk being our top priority. In the end, I understood that it is easy to accept the possibility that the Original Hebrew Israelites – those who wrote the scriptures that still guide so many sectors of Judeo-Christian ways – were a melanated group.

It is a lot more difficult, however, for white Jews to recognize the harm of our Greco-Roman traditions of painting the pictures of the people in these stories as low-melanated. It is more difficult to accept that our religions – meant to teach and remind us of our morals, ethics and how to attain social harmony – have been tainted by desires to control and dominate. And it is challenging to go beyond acceptance of these truths and be comfortable speaking about them to others.

Let's face it: Black folk are our Gods (Just hear me out before you criticize)

Starting with the origins of civilizations and acknowledging the black roots of white power may seem like a stretch, but it remains incredibly important. Why is that? Well, not acknowledging the truth creates a mental and emotional block that hinders us from accepting, discussing, and getting past it. I heard NBA trailblazer Kobe Bryant say that he truly became the best version of himself when he took the time to recognize his weaknesses and work with what he had. The saying that "the truth shall set you free" is not just a cliche statement. It's the only way to move forward.

When we release the constructs that we have learned to use to protect and maintain our images, there is a sense of freedom and relief that allows us to grow and develop in connection to other humans and the planet. We finally can perform at our peak. I have told white folks in these spaces that I feel a level of freedom and I want to share that with others in hope of inspiring others. Many of the responses have often been that they felt like I am saying that they are not free, and they took offense to this. If you feel like I am telling you that you are not free simply by me saying that I want to share my sense of freedom, then maybe you are telling on yourself. Why not – instead of taking offense – be open to a new and different perspective and try to understand where I'm coming from?

If we acknowledge the high melanin levels of the humans whose scriptures we follow, it automatically frees them and us. We can still find the same value in following these great stories to guide our lives. By learning to celebrate those ideas of what our construct of God actually looked like (in books, movies, art, etc.), we will increase the value we place on black lives today. We should be able to acknowledge the great contributions of blacks to the success of our nation. Until we can straight up say 'Our Gods are also Black,' then we cannot be free ourselves. Even if you wish to argue back that maybe not all of them are black, the fact is that we have not acknowledged how our vision about God and our gods is skewed to push the idea of white supremacy. We cannot see the gains we would achieve by supporting others' greatness and aligning ourselves with the fight for justice.

When we identify and celebrate the contributions of black people, we can truly see how uplifting the greatness of other cultures will mean a greater, safer and healthier life for every one of us. Black culture has had a tremendous influence on American culture and other cultures worldwide. Nike knows this, Coca-Cola knows this, General Motors knows this, and many of the large advertising firms know this. If the rest of us acknowledge this, then we can be a part of the solution, help spread the wealth, and support black creators.

I'm Guilty [Breakout Box]

In my attempt to educate others, I realized I was 100% guilty of committing one of the most annoying offenses of woke whiteness. Too many times, I became the progressive super-man asshole who knew-it-all and was never satisfied until people reached my level of "enlightenment." I wish I could say I had the patience to "meet people where they are at" and hear them out. Still, my need to correct and redirect often took over. I justified this by truly believing that my thought process was the best way to move forward. In hindsight, being right or holding the deeper philosophical keys all the time is not very inspiring to others. I, like so many woke folk, have to stop lecturing, start listening, and walk along with people through the process that already exists. This takes time and dedication.

The truth of history is still hard to accept

I met whites who were doing a lot of the work but did not want to regularly attend the discussion groups or general planning meetings because they felt like they didn't have the patience. I also struggled with this same issue. Without some of these folks being present for these more layered sessions, it became almost impossible for some of the regular attendees to grapple with how much our day-to-day actions and systemic structures are a part of white culture - and how harmful and exclusive these structures are to others. What I have repeatedly found is that if we're not talking about blatant and overt racism such as police killings then people are not moved by more nuanced conversations concerning history, the legacy of slavery, and history of white privilege.

Further, in all-white spaces, when I say something from experience and research, without black folks present to express themselves, these statements would often be ignored or dismissed as me overreacting or talking about conspiracy. I saw this as a roadblock in my ability to contribute positively. Not having enough interaction with black folks in the group to support these arguments became a challenge to having critical breakthrough moments. Over time, I realized that I'm a real outsider even in these white anti-racism spaces and that a lot of folks aren't ready to accept a relentless focus on supporting black lives.

Finding a home in anti-racism

Fortunately, I found a home within two groups of the WP4BL. One was established when several organizations joined to fight the building of two new jails in LA. The larger organization was called Justice LA. I felt comfortable as it was more than a protest group. They focused also on educating the general population on the prison system. Our most exciting efforts occurred when we committed a significant amount of brainwork to reimagining how the billions of tax-dollars spent on prisons could be better spent to reduce the need for those jails.

We came up with great plans to achieve specific goals and have already achieved our first goal in halting the investment in the new jails. There are many proposed actions for the redistribution of the $3.5 billion in allocated funds. Unfortunately, I left LA to return to St. Louis before seeing this through. I could not be happier with the present successes of Justice LA and the level of participation by WP4BL members.

The other group that I enjoyed was a smaller group of WP4BL based on geographic location. We were the Mid-city to downtown group. There were about seven of us. Each subgroup had to develop their own mission, vision and work. Our mission was to join other organized allies to bring the voice of racial justice to their lens of social justice. The main two organizations we focused on were the DSA-LA and Revolution LA, which later became Public Bank LA. Public Bank LA addressed the way the City government managed its funds and the city's banking relationship with Wells Fargo.

Our subgroup of WP4BL found that these organizations valued the ideas of BLM and racial justice. We built bonds within those organizations, and they grew to see us as a voice for racial equity. Over time participants of this subgroup moved in and out of the area. Later, I moved to St. Louis and lost touch with them. However, I did see improvement in the language and approach of both DSA-LA and Public Bank LA in their work with BLM and other organizations.

I do believe in white anti-racism organizations

At the risk of the blind leading the blind, complacency and pride, and the natural exclusion of cultural differences, white anti-racism collectives still serve a valuable starting point for whites. Initially, when repairing the harm done, we white folks have naturally decided to work on ourselves to gain comfort in the healing process. When white folks showed up at BLM-LA meetings, I loved how a portion of the meetings were done separately so that the members of each group could focus on themselves and without the pressure of explaining themselves to another race. Having white spaces to work on how to be anti-racist is so important. That's why, despite my struggles, I believe in white anti-racism groups.

Many white folks going through an awakening or who are entering these spaces can feel ashamed, especially the more they learn about the past and the effects of the system's intentional design. Hopelessness and embarrassment can be less intimidating when you're surrounded by fellow whites who will be less harmed than blacks by any mistakes in the learning process. Most importantly, it is often reiterated in these spaces that it is not the responsibility of the people whom we have harmed to help us repair ourselves. That revelation is critical. The work all whites have to do is a serious inside job first.

That is why I continue to work with white anti-racists. It is one of the more powerful ways that I can be aligned with my purpose. Often, parents of young children in these spaces have thanked me for sharing my experience of having been raised inclusively and involved in the black community. In addition, people appreciate my ability to connect knowledge of historical events that demonstrate a consistent pattern of behavior. Most resonate with the many racist experiences of my friends and me that I've shared. White people seem to understand it better when it's coming from a white perspective.

In these groups, I also get a chance to learn how to communicate with progressive white people. I am learning patience and a level of compassion for those who don't share my same experiences. I am very appreciative of those who are dedicated to this work and elated that I am not alone on this journey. It is beautiful to know that my stories of working with children or adults in the black community or through activism has had such a positive effect on white people's lives. Katt Williams was 100% correct when he told us that we need us some black friends.

I know that I need to improve in making the connection with other whites involved in this work. I also see my role as making sure that we do not become complacent. This battle is for the long haul and many times I have observed that these spaces can become comforting to those who feel bad about our history. That comfort often leads people to feeling that they have a home for their emotions and sense of being. This is great if it leads to strengthening their support for reparative action. If it just leads to a feeling of 'I am no longer a racist,' then we have only scratched the surface. And this level of arrogance can be potentially more harmful because they may no longer seek to be a part of the change that is needed, since they feel as if they made it to the other side.

Conclusion of My Life Stories Transitions to My Steps

As I mentioned in my story, I have always wanted to know why racism exists. How can we grow up to make predetermined judgments about a group of human beings that we do not have any experience with as equals thus leading us to causing them harm? So, I spent years observing us, listening to our stories, seeing how we approach situations and how we show up in conversations. In my early adulthood, I envisioned that my path to fulfilling my purpose was to gain power by becoming an insider, whether through the bank or as the business manager of Nelly. It was all about positioning myself to be able to have economic influence. That shifted after I went to Israel for the first time. That trip created a desire to be a servant to a community of humans that were designing a world that I wanted to see exist.

During these years, I got a chance to reflect on a deeper level on how I showed up. I could no longer use my privilege as I once planned to navigate inside a world that was built for me. I am constantly learning to adjust to demonstrating greater humility and being open to other perspectives even if I believe I have the answer. I also learned to admire the truth about how peaceful and connected a world led by aboriginal human beings could potentially be. More so than ever before I wanted to be a part of a humane community. My journey took me through a level of personal struggle that I had not previously experienced. I saw the differences in how our financial state influences our decisions. I was able to experience what I knew to be true, that one can gain knowledge, but understanding comes from experiencing and applying that knowledge.

Until I went through my personal struggle, I did not realize how much being broke in this system is a deterrent from living your personal dreams and goals. From the courses of my PsyD, I learned how important the values, vision and mission are in creating an organization. I could compare the values, vision, and mission of these two worlds (the visions of what the KOY could be and the colonized world that currently exists) – one in an infancy stage with such potential to be sustainable based on the creative power of connectivity to earth and universal laws, and the other on its downfall based on the disconnection to the earth designed for personal control, separation and consumption. I was finally ready to tell my story.

Over and over, I have heard some white folks start a sentence, "I am not racist, but...". I have seen some white folks with the best of desires to help, only to struggle to understand why the people they are trying to help do not follow what they say or even care to listen to them. I watch some too often have an answer and that answer may fit into their vision of the world, but it does not connect with the audience. And I have heard many learn about our privilege and be comfortable speaking about the problems amongst ourselves and too fearful of making mistakes when trying to get involved. I am encouraged though by the amount of white folks who want to see change.

Partially that change is coming anyway because as each generation learns newer information and has more integrated experiences, the shift in how we interact with one another will continue to take place. As Deepak Chopra said on Jimmy Fallon shortly after the Trump election, these are exciting times of chaos brought on by the nature of the change process. He used heating water as an example. The boiling of the water is chaotic as the gas replaces the liquid form. I hope that we continue to push through our societal chaos with the ability to know the potential transformation we can create in our world in how we live and co-exist harmoniously.

I do not have all the answers, and I know that this is not an absolute destination type of solution. What I am sharing with you next are my theories and revelations that have come from conversations with black and brown humans as well as other whites who have been influenced by black and brown humans. I only hope that reading it from the voice of a fellow white man may help reach something in you that you may not otherwise be ready to hear from a person of color.

While the order of the steps has some importance, we will find ourselves using the steps in a combination of ways and they are not strictly sequential. For example, in Step 1 we are not taking action but rather learning to question why things are the way they are and what motivates us. This line of questioning can be applied as we acknowledge our harm and the value of others. Letting go can also be applied hand-in-hand with any of the steps as we learn to be better. The steps are meant to be compatible with one another.

This will not be as easy to read as my personal stories and it may not all sink in. I hope that you will push through and judge for yourself after you have read the entire seven steps. I look forward to the continued conversations that these steps can provide with the hope that the conversations lead to a greater sense of confidence in a world we are motivated to co-create. I want us all to strive to be the best version of ourselves. It is achievable once we truly go through the healing process. Thank you for joining me in this search for a peaceful, joyful, and just world.

Step 1

Don't Move – Seek Understanding

Racism was created by white folks for us. Racism was created by those in power in order to maintain that power. It was a divide-and-conquer strategy so the poorer class would not unify and overthrow the ruling class that were greatly outnumbered. Once established, we continued to perpetuate it because we benefitted from it. It is a weapon of colonialism that helped create a system of privilege and oppression. In this system, we are in a position where we don't have to question its design because it works for us. So, Step 1 is to stop and not take a step at all. Rather than action, it is a call to pause and seek understanding.

It is simple in concept, yet the desire to make a difference right now is real and therefore makes Step 1 a challenge. Not only is it upon us to consciously see our world through the eyes of those who have suffered for our privilege, it is imperative that we understand the inner workings of our own white insecurity. If not, we will likely continue to miss the chance to bring forth the depth of positive transformation we need for it to be meaningful and long lasting. This idea is consistent with Stephen Covey's habit of "Seek first to understand, then to be understood" from his book *The 7 Habits of Highly Effective People*, as well as the Pyramid of Change from the

Arbinger Institute's *Anatomy of Peace*, in which you build relationships, seek understanding and develop improved communication in order to support people and help things go right.

At the root of racism is a lack of humanity

I see racism as the largest-scaled form of bullying. We whites wanted to exploit and control resources that we did not have access to from the regions inhabited by aboriginal and indigenous humans. But rather than working collaboratively with resource-rich people, we violently took what we wanted without any appreciation for those who are indigenous to these lands. We could not even recognize the fact that native humans living in these areas of richness were willing to share it with us.

Pause for a second. Have you ever been in a situation where you were so intensely focused on what you wanted that you went to take it without realizing that it was being offered? Have you ever been so consumed with getting a result that you didn't pay attention to the effects of the manner in which you went about getting it? We all have. If we aren't stopped and forced to recognize the humanity of others, then we are going to continue this process of destruction.

As white people, our actions grow like "the butterfly effect." This theory states that a flap of a butterfly's wing can create a hurricane on the other side of the planet if nothing is there to stop the momentum of the wind created from the original flap of the wing. This is often used as a metaphor to describe unhindered momentum in any form. The force grows to the point that correcting it later becomes more complicated and needs more intentional effort.

This is where we as white people are now. We could not recognize the humanity in others, nor in ourselves, and thus, we became the Earth's biggest bullies. In order to alter this, we must go deeper into why whites have created racism as the main operating agenda across the world. We have to be intentional about understanding this in order to slow harmful ripples of our actions.

Answering the "Why'

It is great to want society to be fair and just. However, I would caution you that fixing the problem is not as straightforward as it seems. The change we bring forth may be effective or may continue to have a negative impact depending on our ability to recognize what truly needs to be modified. This is what Step 1 is about. It allows us to examine what's underneath the surface of racism. In essence, it allows us to first look at the *Why* of racism.

Why did we feel that perpetuating a world that gives us the upper hand was necessary?

Why were we taught to believe that our skin tone made us superior?

As we start with the *Why*, I encourage you to watch Simon Sinek, author and inspirational speaker, explain what motivates us to move. In his TEDx talk, "Start with the Why," he briefly discusses the anatomy of the brain and how we are not driven to action by our knowledge of "the what." Rather, we make decisions and act based on how we feel or as he puts it "the why."

Therefore, as we approach changing from a race-based society to a humanistic society we need to know why we have a racist society. What is the root cause? And, in making the transformation, can the idea of creating a humanistic society be the driving force?

It is only by answering these *whys* that we can finally move past our default logic and habits and into the most inner and effective part of ourselves.

Racism is bullying

The *why* of racism can be traced to white insecurity. We know that individual bullying comes from feelings of insecurity and unresolved or unaddressed pain. Insecurity comes from a feeling or combination of feelings of being less than or from fear. Fears are driven by the unknown, the negative what-ifs. What does that have to do with racism? We developed a feeling that led to a movement based on the thought that our skin tone was a superior skin tone - when in truth our skin is lacking something that is important. Melanin.

We were not painted a color called white. Our color was not an evolutionary improvement from a darker shade of skin. And we don't have the characteristics of the original human beings that spawned all other skin complexions. It's just the opposite. Our skin lacks a pigmentation found in aboriginal and indigenous humans that absorbs sunlight and allows folks to be outside. This means that our skin color actually poses a disadvantage because sunlight is a key factor to life. Being outside in the sun is how we remain connected to the planet. Our low level of melanin could be described as a physical impediment in that our skin will burn faster than those who have a deeper level of melanin.

What does having low melanin mean to us? It means that we can't be out in the sun for long. This was even more of a disadvantage hundreds and thousands of years ago before we had buildings, planes, trains and automobiles or before we had air conditioning and SPF 50 lotions. We had to make decisions based on survival because of our lower levels of melanin.

For whatever reasons we ended up populating areas of the Earth to the North where having less melanin could have an advantage during the colder season. We may have lost our melanin because we moved further away from the equator. We may have moved there to survive not having as much melanin from birth. What I know is that we heavily occupy the northern regions. Just imagine the internal feelings this would lead to as everyone else could spend more time outside. Do you remember when you were a child wanting to play outside before video games ruled our world? Could this have led to jealousy and envy?

What else might have been happening back then that led to the white supremacy approach to win and control at all costs? In these regions, due to less sunlight and colder temperatures, what were the crops like? We know that the proper vegetation our bodies needed to grow did not exist in abundance in these northern regions. It is well documented that the diseases we spread were the largest contributor to conquering the humans occupying the lands that are now controlled by European colonialism. The root of the word dis-ease is to be not at ease. Disease occurs when our body's nutrients and needs are not balanced. Obviously, if we live in lands that do not have all of the natural resources that we need, then it can easily be assumed that we would have more disease.

Could this be where we developed a zero-sum mentality and saw the world as having a limited amount of resources? I believe so. The zero-sum mentality is the belief that there is a finite amount of resources and in order for me to have a larger share, others must give up a portion of theirs. It is based on an idea of scarcity of resources that we need. Without knowledge that the rest of the planet even exists, could we have developed a scarcity mentality and not even understood that this development took place? Could this have led to cultural differences between us and those who had melanin in how we approach survival and managing our day-to-day lives?

Sure, if they occupy areas with more than enough resources, they attain an abundant mindset where sharing is welcome. Is the scarcity mentality where the desire to conquer and control came from? Maybe we just need a hug from each other and to be told that we are deserving of love. (Donald Trump seems to understand this need. He gains the trust of his loyal followers in part by telling them how great and loved they are).

When we journeyed to other lands maybe we were ostracized, told how pathetic we are for not having melanin, and that we are not worthy of having these resources. But that doesn't fit the characteristics of people of color. Could we not see that indigenous and aboriginal groups such as black and brown folks are more than willing to share?

We know that in this territory we named America from the journal writings of Christopher Columbus, Europeans were met with sharing and giving humans who we chose to attempt to destroy rather than appreciate. Rather than learn from those we encountered in other lands how to enjoy being connected to the earth, we enslaved peaceful indigenous humans, forcing them to build our infrastructures, raise our crops, and serve our needs. We abused their bodies for our own personal gain. We developed systems based on deception in an effort to justify our behavior.

Christopher Columbus wrote about how willing the native humans were to share their resources. Sharing was an obvious choice since the earth provided these resources. They did not belong to humans. Europeans could have been grateful. Yet, Columbus wrote about how we wanted to take and control the people and the resources of this area.

In his book *Lies My Teacher Told Me*, James W. Loewen wrote about the desires for domination among European countries during that time, which influenced Columbus and others to change their thoughts about and emotions towards the beautiful and kind people of the new lands. Because they wanted to control the resources and enslave the people for their own greed, they called them savages and heathens (since they didn't convert to Christianity). There were more than enough resources for everyone and yet he and the rest of European culture could not see that there was no need to dominate in order to have what they wanted.

My friend Chevela often says, "People are so used to dysfunction that they don't know what function is." Because we have not dealt with this internal misconception of the scarcity mentality and the fears that it creates, we continue to practice those traits thereby perpetuating dysfunction. Even though those who had all of the resources we needed were willing to share with us and we would have no longer been in need, our scarcity mentality wouldn't allow us to see and accept this truth. Instead, we decided to conquer in our determination to dominate. This is where the win at all cost mentality stems from. Dr. Claud Anderson, author and economist, teaches us that the term race came from the race of European countries to dominate lands and resources.

Still today, we operate from a scarcity zero sum mentality. We have more than enough vegetation and resources to feed the Earth's entire population a healthy diet and provide a comfortable home. Yet, we have people starving and unhoused. International corporations fight to dominate the world we live in. In fact, "dominate" is one of Amazon.com's core values taught to employees. This is one of the feelings that drove us before and it still drives us today. We are in a race and it's all about winning.

Don't take a step

The reason why we don't begin with taking a step is because we must recognize that we never learned why we became a culture that created and maintained racism in the first place. In essence, we never grappled with the fundamental insecurity that was the driving force behind colonialism.

For all my fellow progressives who are trying to correct our wrongs, words are not enough, showing up to protest is not enough and voting for someone is not enough. They are often welcomed components. However, if this is the limit to our level of participation, then how can we expect the transformation to happen?

We need to share space with those folks who do not agree with the need to modify our system and have difficult conversations. Sometimes that will take leaving conversations unresolved, knowing that we have planted seeds. How we continue to build upon those moments is important. For those people of color we are attempting to support, we must go through the process of learning how we can be most helpful by offering ourselves and finding out how we can best serve. It will take time and repetition to gain trust and improve relations.

We need to check our egos when we ask ourselves, "Why am I getting involved?" Whatever reasons we join the efforts to change, we should remain aware that this is not about us. I am not suggesting that we ignore our personal desires to be a part of the transformation. I am suggesting that we remain aware that we can show up and leave the fight for justice anytime we want because of our privilege to ignore the living conditions of other lives and communities. This journey is not something that others can leave and not think about the impact of how they experience and are experienced by our practices. Black folks continually have to alter their approach to fit in enough to survive. Therefore, we must alter our approach to achieve change, given that this is what we truly desire.

How we show up is important. This is why the first step of identifying our foundation of our culture is so important. Our willingness to accept that we should not dictate the relationships with people of color, and that we do not have to have all the right answers is important. In watching how our leaders have shown up, I witnessed Bernie Sanders and Elizabeth Warren be examples of missing opportunities. For as much as I love Bernie for his fight against systemic injustice, he shows up as a white man with all the answers far too much. He missed many great opportunities to show humility and ask questions to black folks about what is needed. Although he improved from 2016 to 2020 Bernie could have learned more about how he can offer support and encourage others to do the same.

When he was willing to hear those who experienced the harm from our social systems and culture, he was able to consider things that he had not previously thought of as a white male. That level of curiosity is invaluable. It demonstrates respect that others know what is best for themselves. Too often Bernie spoke as if he had the answers. Given the history of white men showing up that way, I think he missed opportunities to gain the trust needed to create his vision even after his perspective modified.

For as much as I respect Elizabeth Warren and believe her heart and efforts are well intended to create healing, she missed a great opportunity of humility when her DNA test results showed that she was not as closely related to the indigenous humans as she thought. Beyond an apology and stating that her grandmother raised her to believe this fact, she could have talked about why she valued that idea. What is it about the indigenous culture and the people with whom she thought she had a tribal connection that she cherished and wants to see more of in our world? I believe this would have helped her in a couple of ways. First it would have altered the appearance that she was using being a part of indigenous culture to gain some political credit. Secondly, it would have demonstrated that there are values in indigenous cultures that we should be aware of and appreciate.

I found in both cases, Bernie and Elizabeth were too defensive and so were many of their followers that I spoke to. There is a difference between explaining what you have to offer and allowing others to make decisions versus coming in with the answers for someone else's life. I'm not saying that all melanated humans will automatically have the solutions either, but they deserve to make decisions and learn from their mistakes, just as we do, especially when the results directly affect their lives and their communities.

When we show up, all of us are symbols of the oppressive history of our people, whether or not we (or our ancestors) have directly participated in creating or perpetuating this system. As we look to have an impact, without awareness of how we show up, then we will continue the harm because we are too focused on us. It will show. Stepping back means for us to allow things to happen without us controlling the outcome. It is a great opportunity for us to observe and serve as needed.

That's the primary reason that the Step 1 is not to take a step. Rather, we must learn how to recognize the mentality, emotions, intentions, and behaviors that created and maintained this system and lifestyle. Our low levels of melanin may not biologically have a direct effect on our mental or physical abilities to act and perform as two legged mammals. But I would argue that the behaviors that white people have practiced are driven by winning a race that we subconsciously feel insecure and fearful about losing.

Furthermore, for us to heal our racism, we must enter a process of letting go. Let's reflect on how we got here before we can shift our direction. Let's prepare ourselves for effective action that leads to lasting positive transformation.

In the void of doing nothing is the opportunity to start on Steps 2 and 3. This takes continuous effort to unlearn with an understanding that we, and generations before us, have been greatly deceived. We must stop and get ready to learn from a new set of teachers.

Step 2

Acknowledge the Harm

What was presented in Step 1 describes what the Kingdom of Yah calls an injured mind. In this case, our injured mind stems from a loss of connection to the earth, which I believe is because our melanin levels prevented us from surviving in sunnier warmer conditions. Our minds led us consciously and subconsciously to create a world through our outward behaviors and continuous practices. The conscious effort is to dominate the world, to win the race, if you may. The subconscious effort is to protect ourselves in this world we are creating by defending our decisions and working to prevent the harm we think exists in a scarce world.

I believe that, in a world of meritocracy, we most fear being exposed for the inconsistencies between how we believe we will be able to perform and what we're taught (our deeper insecurities despite being taught superiority). Our ego is at risk. Therefore, we outwardly behave in efforts to maintain control in a position of power and privilege. These behaviors become our practices.

A common response today when asked how you are doing is, "I can't complain." Even though we all have complaints. No matter what your values, goals, and desires are, most of us acknowledge that this world we created is not just. Yet we are stuck in a cycle of trying to maintain it while wanting the results to reflect the desired differences we seek. There is a saying that "hurt people hurt people." In this case, I would argue that our injured mind has hurt all life on this planet. Therefore, white culture, which stems from this injured mind, is at the root of many of our issues.

Even for those of us who want America to go back to "the good old days," or those who are upset by immigration and social programs that are designed to uplift other groups of people, we feel a sense of harm due to the zero-sum mentality. I got news for you. White folks are causing the harm. White culture leads us to believe that someone else's progress is a threat to ours. Even if that is true (which it's not), then it is by design because a desire to win automatically creates a desire for others to lose. We feel like we need have-nots in order to be in the group of haves. It is an injured mind that wants others to suffer in order to feel like the people with the injured mind have accomplished something.

As in the case with any injury, we need repair. Repairing an injured mind occurs by consciously following the first five steps in this book. Repair begins through an acknowledgement of the injury and the harm that we are causing. That is what this step is about. In acknowledging the harm of our ways, we must also acknowledge the value of those we have targeted in our bully-like practices. Next comes Step 3, which is a process of letting go.

Then, in Step 4, we must learn to appreciate and be comfortable giving credit to melanated humans. This is followed by repairing the harm we have inflicted on aboriginal and indigenous humans. Then we can truly begin building our new world. In doing so, through the process of the first five steps, we can allow a different mind to lead us towards the last step, humanity.

The intentions to harm

In Step 2, I focus on two key elements of how our culture developed. One element is related to anti-black racism and the other is related to our desire to play God. As we experience Step 2, I want to remain focused on the psychology of our white culture. We must examine the approach and intentions of what we created and how our behaviors maintain it. In Step 2, we focus on learning and acknowledging the numerous intentional efforts by whites to destroy black humans and black folks' attempts to build community.

For example, we have learned about the overt violence of the enslavement of African people. What most of us did not learn is that the intentions were to affect their minds. Beating someone does not force them to do what you want. No, our enslavement was deliberately planned and took a significant amount of effort. We physically bred Aboriginals to create babies that were separated from their families with the intention of creating interchangeable parts that we would use, abuse, and discard like any other property. We raised babies to fear us and rely on us so that as they became older, they wouldn't think about leaving. If they did leave, they were violently beaten and or hung publicly to make examples of them. We raped the women to display our power. If a baby resulted, then we raised our own child as our slave.

This quick explanation displays a very intentional mindset that is violent and ill beyond the scope of the physical violence we learned about in school textbooks. Imagine, we are God fearing, religious white folks that did all of this. We wanted a world built for ourselves and had to convince ourselves that we are worthy of having others build this world for us. Now ask yourself, do you see the traits of this mentality still today?

Slavery existed for over 200 years in America and yet we learn very little about it. Two hundred years of black chattel slavery that launched this nation into a powerhouse for the benefit of Europeans and all we learn about it and its aftermath takes up a few pages in our history textbooks growing up. So, you say I'm sick of talking about slavery. It ended in its legal form over 170 years ago. Then let's attempt to repair the harm we've done. Otherwise, we keep repeating the same intentions because we never get to the cause: our injured mind.

Anti-black racism

Throughout our history, even up to today, as black communities have tried to establish their own lives in our world, why have white people heartlessly attempted to destroy their progress and limit their opportunities? Burning churches, burning and bombing black business districts, and for what? Were we defending ourselves? Why were prominent black leaders such as Medgar Evers and Martin Luther King, Jr. killed? Because they wanted economic justice. They never said let's attack those kind white folks who are minding their own business. So what is our real excuse? Sit with that for a moment.

The only answer I see is that we are more naturally prone to violence. Add in the deceptive ways of Co-Intel Pro, white flight, the predatory financial practices, and the limitation of resources and access to quality food, health care, and opportunities. This type of mind wants to create such a level of hopelessness for another group of people, with whom we are barely familiar, knowing that these conditions would lead to violence and self-destruction. Reflect on our thought process that wants to destroy a people or have them destroy themselves and then to create a false narrative about them to make them seem as if they are violent and vile by nature.

The need for niggers

To examine our anti-black racism, I want to go back to the why. To quote James Baldwin in his 1963 interview with Kenneth B. Clark "What white people have to do, is try and find out in their own hearts why it was necessary to have a nigger in the first place, because I'm not a nigger, I'm a man, but if you think I'm a nigger, it means you need it and you got to find out why. The future of the country depends on that." While we have tried to eliminate the use of the N-word from our vocabulary, we have not addressed the issue Baldwin presents. It is difficult to have corrective measures take place until we understand the motivating factors.

Nigger is a violent term, and it represents a low-melanated people's level of violence towards aboriginal people. Why are we so violent towards aboriginal humans? Answering this includes taking into full consideration the pure hatred mentality that we developed. It takes examining the level of mental illness that would violently exploit people. It takes examining how we implement this violence, with intentions to harm and consistently hold back indigenous humans over the course of the entire time we conceived this nation until now.

As I stated in the Step 1, these are traits of a jealous and envious mindset. It is commonly known in the black community that the view of white folks is that "we hate you because we ain't you." I am open to hearing other possibilities since I was not in this body when this movement began. Yet, jealousy and envy cause the types of actions that begin with harming someone you have not met, especially when you want what they have.

So, does this mean that we want melanin? Well, many of us certainly want tanner skin every chance we get. But deeper than that, we wanted to be able to access the earth's natural resources. We wanted to grow, cultivate and manage our own resources. We wanted buildings and cities created for us to live and function. We wanted to create societies that operated with a flow of exchanging energy and resources. One question is, did we know how to do so on our own after we recognized it being done elsewhere? I would say no, or we would have simply done so for ourselves.

Because of developing a scarcity mentality, when we saw groups who looked different from us, we chose to steal what they had, and or force them into making what we wanted. The Greco-Romans went into Egypt and Jerusalem and other areas of Africa and learned with a desire to steal and conquer. During the Moorish conquest in Europe which began in 711, it was black and brown Moors who built European's era-defining infrastructures before Europeans came to the western continents. Yet, as Europe's most violent criminals raced to the Americas, we created a more violent display of who we are and a system of racism.

Lies and deceit

So, how do we convince a world that our skin tone makes us superior, especially when it does not? We lie. We say that not having a pigmentation in your skin that absorbs one of the providing sources of life makes you a better human being. Then we lie about lying and lie about why we are lying just as the Latter-Day Saints warned us would happen in their 1980s anti-lying commercial. We created a world founded on deception.

For a lie to be effective you need an audience. If I tell you a lie about a stranger that you have not met, something that you would not have a clue if it is true or not, out of the three people involved you are the most likely to be deceived by the lie. The human being lied about will know it is not true. I will know it's not true. So white people, that means that we have been deceived the most. We have been taught lies about aboriginal and indigenous human beings, lies that we would not have believed if we didn't want to feel that we were inherently better.

Here is an example of the magic show of lies. Tim Wise, who speaks on issues of racism, early in his speech titled "Pathology of Privilege: Racism, White Denial & The Cost of Inequality" talking about how the media portrays the death of black folks in this country. We were not told by the media about how the American Journal of Public Health published in 2004 a report based on a study of ten years from 1991 to 2000 of over 1 million black folks that "died essentially because of their blackness" and the conditions that the majority are forced to live in.

He points out that this is an academic journal that put time and research into this article. The authors demonstrate how these same folks would not have died, living in white areas that have less environmental toxicity and average health care considering what various white folks receive. Yet he points out that it is very uncommon for any of us to get our news from such a source. Only doctors, other professionals, and few others read such a journal.

Tim continues by asking, "How is over 1 million dead black folks not news?" He says, "We do find out from the media when a white supremacist murders a black man and rightfully, we should. We hear about hate crime murders of individuals and well we should. But when one million human beings die from systemic injustice, we do not hear one word of it." This is why what we have *not* been taught harms us more than what we are taught. Would knowing this have led to change? I do not know. Would it have led to us asking more questions about why this is happening and what can be done? I would like to think the answer is yes.

However, the question remains, what are the intentions in not letting the public know? One intention is to continue to harm black folks for the sake of our own hierarchical gains. A second intention is to keep us ignorant of the facts so that we can be used to maintain the status quo. We are a weapon to continue the harm. For us to be used most effectively, we must remain ignorant, arrogant, fearful, confused, distant, distracted, ill, and angry. Each one of these emotions can be used to further the agenda of maintaining white supremacy culture.

Imagine, given this form of deception that Tim Wise discussed, a practice that continues into the 2000s and beyond, then how can we expect our teaching in school about our history to be any different? I believe that the lack of honesty that we practice in how we tell our story is the reason why we still remain unhealed as a nation and as a world. Just as our oppressive culture benefited from teaching melanated children they are inferior and low-melanated children that they are superior, avoiding the teaching of our intentions and the results of not repairing the damage leaves children to grow into adulthood not understanding how we got here and what to fix.

Conspiracies or conspiracy theories

We allow for industry leaders and government agencies to use deceptive methods to gain control and cause harm while creating an alternative narrative that hides the truth. This is reflected in our food management and healthcare systems. There is no doubt that European culture has brought forth illnesses and profited heavily from our food management, drugs, and health care systems. We do not teach the truth about how what we eat impacts our minds, bodies, and energy.

We have commercials – such as those for children's cereals – that lie to us about the nutrients in the products. Companies are not required to inform us in their commercials that these products are made from chemicals and processes that make us unhealthy. We use profits to defend our decisions and create the illusion of freedom of choice to make decisions that result in self-harm. But within that choice should be a freedom of knowledge so that our choices are self-affirming. Not doing this takes conspiring.

Conspiring has consistently been implemented in the racism that exists with the omitted history from our textbooks being only one example. It has also been a major component of how our so-called justice system and economic systems have used their power to create such high levels of hopelessness and violence in black communities. Take Co-Intel Pro and the War on Drugs. The CIA, FBI and local law enforcement agencies were instrumental in targeting the black community with drugs and guns to both destroy those communities and finance their other intentions such as the Iran Contra Affair.

From redlining to unfair credit practices, the financial and real estate industries have conspired to make blacks appear less valuable. Each of these examples took coordinated efforts that have been exposed in more recent years although with much less publicity than I believe it should have received. These efforts still continue today in various shapes and forms for the same reasons that Tim Wise raised his questions. If we ignore these problems, they do not go away. The question is do we want them to or not?

With the access to video editing and distribution along with the analytics and data gathering used for targeting audiences, conspiracy theories of all sorts have taken on a new and expanded life of their own. Government and large corporations conspiring together has been woven into our practices for so long. To dismiss groups of people as crazy for believing that conspiring is taking place is dangerous, especially when we only use the far-fetched theories to justify shutting folks down. We must acknowledge that there is a reason that we are willing to believe conspiracy theories in the first place. We must begin to address pulling the curtain back on the "Wizard of Oz" of our white world.

China

The new colonizers of the world are China. They took the playbook and are implementing it now with the goal of becoming the new world-dominating culture. Reportedly, their methods to grow their wealth were based on many years of low income work and horrible working conditions. Business owners gained great wealth from many low waged workers. That is the way to grow your economy, until the wealth accumulation amongst the few can begin to expand globally.

China is now using their wealth to create loans for African countries to develop infrastructure. According to various news reports, the Chinese are controlling how the loaned money is being managed and not allowing the African nations and their citizens to control their own growth and development. When the loans that were set up to be unpayable go into default, the resources of these countries become the collateral for the defaulted loans.

In *Confessions of an Economic Hitman,* John Perkins described how our Greco-Roman culture did the same. The International Monetary Fund and World Bank were created by Europe and the US for the benefit of our international corporations. He describes how he would act as an economic hitman to create plans for countries to take loans for developing their roads and electrical grids. The plans falsely show how the country could develop its infrastructure and grow its wealth. When the countries were unable to repay those loans, they were either forced to give The US military space to build a base and or give colonizers the control of the natural resources of these lands.

It appears that is many cases, China is duplicating these efforts with the same intentions. Until we make corrections and see the value in a connected world that we do not need to control, the story will keep repeating itself. In this case, it could be a reaction to the exploitation created by the international corporations from Europe and North America that pressured China to maintain low costs. If this is result, this is another example of the oppressed becoming the oppressor.

I am not saying that all Chinese people are part of the problem. My concern is the cultural practice. One thing that China and the Greco-Roman world have in common is that we are both evolved or mutated forms of the aboriginal humans from which we all originate. Just a coincidence? Perhaps. Or it could be that there is something to it that makes us want to rule, whereas aboriginal and indigenous cultures remain connected to the planet and therefore do not want to cause it or the life on earth harm.

Words cannot lead the way to healing

Another harm of deception comes in the confusion it causes. The lack of an absolute language means that the power to define becomes even more of a struggle. I look at us today and observe how so much of our conversation is about how we converse. We are constantly using our language to define our culture. That seems to be a tail wagging the dog. Too often I have been in conversations trying to make a point and, because I am not keeping up with the newest trends in language, instead of discussing the impact of the topic or what can be done, the conversation becomes interrupted by what terminology I use.

Language reflects a thought process and a culture. Language does not solely originate a thought process and develop a culture. Therefore, rather than worrying about being politically correct, let's learn how to be correct. Language can be used to support that process.

The danger is that we keep stopping progress. Emotions can be expressed with exaggerated generalizations. Anger can be expressed with meaningless wishes or idle threats that just needed to be released. Many people who love each other have said hurtful things to each other when angry that express their thoughts and feelings at the moment, even if they are not truly accurate in general.

For example, my mom told me to "Get out! And never come back!" on a number of occasions when I was young and immature and pushed her past her limits. Once we both cooled off, we were able to address the real issues and move forward. If we cannot continue the conversation, how do we heal and connect? If we do not connect, how do we come together? Given that words can have so many meanings it is important to find the connections rather than controlling the semantics narrative. We must continue to develop how we socialize by focusing on the message and not the use of language. Emotions are expressed often by using extreme statements. Judging them as factual or not or by the choice of words skews what is really being expressed.

Suppressing emotions for the sake of getting the expression right for the audience is detrimental. This is certainly a trait that I have struggled with when talking about important issues regarding race. Rather than feeling comfortable expressing myself in my use of language, I have had to argue about the semantics and the point has been lost. I believe we should emphasize the importance of continuing through the struggle of identifying our emotions and allowing for the expression. Otherwise, our emotions may come out in ways that can be more harmful.

For example, ask my father or any of his brothers and they will tell you their father was hard on them as children if not verbally abusive. Grandpa Bob would tell my grandmother how frustrated he was having to play politics and smile and be nice during his daily routine just to accomplish his goals as an attorney. This forced him to suppress feelings for which he would later use family as an escape. It may have been done subconsciously but the emotions found their way out. I have witnessed many examples of how we use the comfort of loved ones, who we trust will be there for us, as our verbal punching bags.

White culture is known for trying to shut off our emotions. "This is business not personal," "Keep your emotions out if it and deal with the facts," or "Never let them see you sweat" are common terms used to do so. This disconnected thought leads to language that suppresses feelings. The term emotions has motion in it. Emote is an active word that should not be held back.

Feelings are within all of us, and their expression will come out either directly or indirectly. Saving face to remain in a position of control and privilege is a pillar of white culture and leads to violence and destruction. If we examine the mental state of any of the mass shooting perpetrators, we will find that their suppressed emotions played a role in leading them to cause great harm. Choosing to separate life from business creates a profit driven world that values the medium of exchange over relationships to life on earth.

It all leads to this new trend in conversation: cancel culture. Yes, cancel culture continues to disconnect us. When I speak of cancel culture, I am not just speaking of the liberal attempts to use political correctness to stop the conversation as previously mentioned. The far right is all about cancelling other cultures, as well. Anything that challenges us to reflect on how we approach others and be accountable for our actions is often ignored and "cancelled." Many on the right often want to deny discussion about our vicious past and even remove teaching about it in our schools. Teaching this subject matter could allow children to react and express their emotions about what they learn and discuss how they would like to proceed in life with this given understanding.

No matter what race, each of us are different in how we communicate and express our emotions. We are triggered and bothered by different stimuli. Given that nothing is permanent – especially our feelings and our conditions – continuing to keep the communication channels open allows for deeper understanding and learning how we can improve. Learning to appreciate the discomfort of allowing others to be different and share a space with these differences is essential to the healing process.

Playing God

As we look at changing our culture, it's one thing to discuss that we are built on a lie called white supremacy. What else are we hiding about our culture that goes beyond racism and includes harm to all humans and even the planet? How about how enrooted in death it is? In the life-giving spirit of creativity, if we all lived like the Messiahs and Gods, and according to the messages of the stories we use in our religions and or spiritual teachings, then we would want each other to be healthy and the most creative beings possible. That is what promoting life means at its highest level of vibration.

Does our feeling of supremacy create the desire to control others and outcomes? Once you bring a desire to control the outcomes of the creative spirit, you eradicate the natural creative energy. You no longer are letting life happen as it will. Therefore, a controlling culture is a death-based culture.

Control is a foundational value to colonial approach. It stems from the scarcity mentality that if you have then I do not. Therefore, I must get for myself in order to control my own destiny. It leads to an individualistic approach that disconnects us. Then we use a deceptive approach to maintain control. The desire for control leads us to what I would refer to as playing God. In our Greco-Roman culture, we make the laws to work for our perceived benefit.

The splitting of the atom which led to our nuclear weaponry is an example of playing God. Robert Oppenheimer was a key member of the Manhattan Project which was a group of scientists who discovered how to split the atom. This discovery was then used to create nuclear weapons. The atom is the smallest unit of an element of life on the planet. By splitting it, one is altering if not destroying that life. This approach means we can determine who and what form of life shall live and who and what shall die. Only a culture that wants to control other forms of life would consider such a drastic approach.

After this discovery and witnessing the plans for use and amount of destruction that came from nuclear weapons, Robert Oppenheimer said, "[W]e have made a thing, a most terrible weapon, that has altered abruptly and profoundly the nature of the world. We have made a thing that, by all standards of the world we grew up in, is an evil thing. And by doing so, by our participation in making it possible to make these things, we have raised again the question of whether science is good for man, of whether it is good to learn about the world, to try to understand it, to try to control it, to help give to the world of men increased insight, increased power. Because we are scientists, we must say an unalterable yes to these questions..."

The same is true about our approach to our food system. We add in the component of capitalism and our disconnection with life rings true in our approach to how we think and use food. For example, insects play a role in a life that exists beyond us as individuals and our desire for convenience. Many Insects eat fruits that have gone rotten, while others feed off the same vegetation we do in its peak form. The idea that there would not be enough if we did not rid ourselves of insects taking over our plant life is a deceptive practice used to justify creating chemical pesticides and genetically modifying these natural plants for our consumption.

Why? The ecosystem exists and works to optimal use for us without our deciding to alter molecular structures. The drugs that we create come from a natural source, but due to our desire to patent and control the outcome, we again change the molecular structure of the source in order to own the patent. Hence we have side effects. Now we have a system that is disconnected from our earth lifecycle and profits from focusing on effects (symptoms) rather than preventing causes. The reality is that our bodies have the magnificent ability to adjust to changes and heal from injury and harm. In addition to that innate ability, the earth and sun provide us what we need for our health and well-being to be optimized.

The problem lies in the desire for power to control. This reflects the intentions of white supremacy culture. Indigenous cultures study science and are very interested in how things work. The approach is to understand that we are a part of life on the planet. Their desire is to be at one with this life, not to control it. This is a fundamental practice that we need to identify in ourselves, learn to let it go and allow the minds of the aboriginal humans, who can feel the rhythm of the earth's vibrations and become part of the flow of energy, guide us to being able to do the same. We must give up our desire for control and our formal structures that we created based on what we knew about the earth back then and become one with the earth now. Surrender, accept and let go.

First, let's admit the harm

In all of our inner work, research and reflection, let us keep in mind that acknowledging the harm of our actions is the necessary first phase to transforming that harm. By acknowledging the harm we inflict, by understanding the role our ancestors played in history, and by examining the implications of our everyday thoughts, behaviors and actions - we finally can heal. We can envision a world free of white supremacy and begin to accept how things may differ once our race and culture is no longer in charge of things.

If acknowledging the harm leads to grief, know that the grieving process triggers the healing process. My close friend Vince who has overcome trauma and works with clients engaged in the healing process explained to me the following:

The natural purpose of grief is for an individual to be able to innately find a place of acceptance. The acceptance one must get to in order to begin the healing of a particular dis-ease is the acceptance of the dis-ease itself and the acceptance of the "self-adjustments" required to initiate the healing process of the dis-ease.

The first stage of grief and, unfortunately, the stage that most people get stuck in is denial/defensiveness. Other stages include anger, bargaining, and depression. However, many of us remain in the stage of denial/defensiveness, which tends to enable a dis-ease to fester and to destroy our lives. Others have problems with the bargaining stage, which can go hand in hand with guilt. If you identify yourself in this stage of grief, try to be gentle with yourself. Note that blame and responsibility are not the same thing. Blaming ourselves or our ancestors for the current situation doesn't help us accept our current situation or our responsibility in the healing process.

Acceptance is a stage some people never get to, especially if they don't allow themselves to experience all the other emotions that come first. By doing the work, we can reach the point of acceptance where we can grow and heal.

Step 3

Letting Go of Privilege, Power and Fear

Earlier in *Race for What*, I discuss how healing racism from within is a lot like diagnosing and healing a severe injury. Answering the *Why* we created racism in Step 1 was the critical diagnostic step. Acknowledging the harm of our culture in Step 2 was the vital piece of accepting the truth and severity of the injury. Now, we must move on to the healing process. Letting go is the beginning of that healing. In Step 3, we will affirm why we must heal and start to release our privilege, power and fear.

The value of letting go for white folk

Letting go is an amazing step because it allows us to open ourselves to greater opportunities that we may not be able to see by holding on to our values, thoughts, feelings, and practices. Letting go is truly freeing, especially because we whites are so focused on our position of superiority in society. We are limited by the constant pressures we place upon ourselves that keep us disconnected from the earth and each other. We have not learned enough about the value of other cultures and how to appreciate their differences. By learning to value letting go, we can experience life from a different perspective. My hope is that we can enjoy the journey of new values, and of reconnecting.

For this seven-step process, letting go allows us to be the best version of ourselves. The late Kobe Bryant once talked about how he allowed himself to be great when he acknowledged his limitations. Once he realized and accepted what he was not, he was able to focus on what he was able to do and work to be the best at that. For me, I wanted to be a football or basketball player when I first learned to love sports, mostly because it was a great way to be with friends. When I learned to accept that I couldn't dunk a basketball without Shando lifting me in the air and that my mother was right, I would get myself killed on the football field, I was free to truly develop other aspects of myself.

In the process of letting go of those dreams, I reflected on why they were so important to me. I realized that I could enjoy being a part of those sports by supporting my friends who played them. I also realized that being with others and supporting others is what made the sports attractive to me. I learned to find other ways to be the best version of myself through community service and helping others develop businesses. I found enjoyment and appreciation for my journey to realize what mattered most to me.

Letting go also provides us opportunities to open ourselves up to experiences that we otherwise would not have allowed ourselves to learn from and enjoy. New perspectives are out there. We can benefit from them if we are able to face fears and let go of what we have been taught to preconceive. There are countless friendships that have developed over the years simply through interactions that would not have existed through continued segregation. When folks accept the differences and are willing to hear each other and celebrate our differences, our values organically change. When we value each other, we cause less harm to one another.

When I learned to let go, I realized that I could share space with racist people. And by sharing space together, we both were able to grow. During my first freshman and only year at Ohio State University, I shared a dorm experience with other young men that had developed very racist mindsets from their childhood. Yet, prior to knowing this about them and them knowing much about me, we developed a bond. As we found out more about each other, we were able to continue to dialogue, learn from and enjoy one another.

I could not believe that I could have racist friends, but they looked out for me and helped in ways I did not expect. Their racist beliefs were only a part of who they were. I was also visited by friends who are black. All of us, black and white were able to interact with one another without talking about race. My white friends became less comfortable with their racism because I was around. When their frat mates would say racist comments, I could see the discomfort and eventually so could their frat mates. The discomfort forced some level of alteration over that year. I only hope that it continued. I know that the change I witnessed was solid enough to build on.

What do we do?

The idea of letting go is not ignoring or suppressing our emotions. It is about recognizing the thoughts that led up to them. Then we give ourselves space to feel them, meanwhile analyzing where the thoughts came from and how we might modify our thoughts in order to feel a different emotion. In doing so, we learn to respond as opposed to react. This is a journey, in which mistakes may happen.

Just remember, no moment is so defining that progress can't be made moving forward. While we work through our fears, what does letting go look like for us in the context of moving into a healed world? To put it simply, I believe rapper Ludacris said it best when he roared, "Move B#$%h, get out the way, get out the way B#$%h, get out the way." That may sound harsh, and it is. But we whites need to get out of our own way. The destruction we have caused is real. We don't have time for our feelings to be in the way of the repair that is close to 200 years overdue.

Letting go means that we must release all of our discomforts, shame, guilt, anger, hate, fear, and insecurity, and on the flip side, let go of leading the way to recovery and feeling like we must have the answers. It goes hand in hand with Step 1. Take a second and look at those emotions. None of them are a way of leading us to a better life. We used our minds that developed from an illusion of scarcity to build this world, a world that we all recognize the need to change and want to change. If we are honest, we must acknowledge that that same mind cannot lead the transformation process because we do not have any practice living the way that we want.

Obstacles to letting go

Despite the value of letting go, there are real obstacles in the way of white people releasing our privilege, power, and fear. First of all, 'letting go' is not something we prioritize in our culture, let alone practice consistently when it comes to power and privilege. Quite the opposite – we are taught to fight to be right, to be the expert, and to be in charge of everything all of the time. Not to mention, we've grown overly accustomed to telling others to let go of thoughts of being damaged from racism.

"Pick yourself up by your bootstraps." "It wasn't me who enslaved you." "Slavery was hundreds of years ago." "Look at all the improvements in integration." "Stop using race as an excuse." I am sure there are others you can think of. At the same time, we are particularly loath to admit that the history of America is steeped in a white mental attitude of superiority that still inflicts us.

Why are we asking those who we have harmed to carry the burden of moving forward in a system that we, who have the power to change, have not changed? Could it be that we don't want to let go of our superior position? Could it be that we have become so accustomed to letting those we have harmed hold the burden of caring for us?

I see the following as the most impactful ways we avoid letting go:

Oppression Olympics: One of the primary ways we avoid letting go is bringing up the harm done to white folks. This is called the 'Oppression Olympics." I have witnessed it in circles of justice organizing. Too often they find themselves having to include and care for all others, rather than just focusing on black folk. Because so many of us struggle in this modern day system, it is easy to see overlap and to call out the suffering of us all. But we must remind ourselves that our skin color has never been systematically used to hold us back from achieving our goals or deployed as the basis for being harmed. Rare situations where this type of harm or discrimination have taken place are isolated. They also do not have a continuous impact because they lack systemic support.

Many of us in lower economic status are also targeted to remain in a lower economic status. Yes - we all hurt from disruptive and oppressive systems. Yet, at the bullseye of these targets is the black community. This means that the system is designed to hurt blacks first and with the greatest impact and then use the same tactics to harm others of low income. Because of this, we must be careful not to act like crabs in a barrel. Rather, we must see the power of letting go, cultivate intentional healing for ourselves, and then step aside to allow the communities we have harmed to cultivate their healing as well.

Fear of not being in control: There are many reasons we may fear changing our culture. Fear of losing control is one of them. We like *our* way of getting what we want, so much so that we often have difficulty dealing with not getting our way. What will a world look like for us if we are no longer in a position of advantage? What do the results of vulnerability look like? As we find ourselves in a position to lose control, it is a natural response to desperately try to cling to or to force our control even further.

I believe we are seeing this now with the older generations of white males who have been in control of this world for so long. Even though we recognize the need for creating a different way, it is deeply scary to go through the process when we are still grappling with our need to control. This reality is addressed in any rehabilitation process dealing with an addiction. For us, our addiction has been trying to control our outcomes and surroundings. Yet, any modifications we make will be cosmetic unless we let go of controlling the change.

False fear: I often hear projected fear that we are worried that blacks may want to act out revenge upon us. Yet, as Katt Williams said in his 2020 Supreme commercial speech "(We) have been waiting 400 years for that to happen." This is why Katt has also said many times that we need friends from other cultures. While writing this book, I was driving a passenger for Uber, a white male in his mid-40s. Otis Redding's *Sitting on the Dock of the Bay* was playing through the sound system from my Pandora station. The passenger told me that he loved this song and he loved black musical artists. We talked about a few who are no longer with us.

To my surprise, he blurted out how much he hated racism. He knew that a few of the artists were assassinated for political reasons. We had a 40-minute drive, so we had time to talk about our views and where we were from in St. Louis. He went to a predominantly white high school that played U. City in basketball. He talked about how we kicked their ass as did many other schools, but he and his friends loved playing basketball because they were able to interact with people who they would not otherwise have had a chance to know.

He then told me he was a Trump supporter and so were his friends. It was around election time, and he was worried how I would react. I told him that I didn't like either candidate. He told me to make sure and tell my friends that there are plenty of Trump supporters who do not like racism or racists and would stand up against racism. The conversation was humming along until suddenly it veered into an irrational fear that frequents the white mind.

He said to me that he wishes he could interact with black folks more, but he was concerned that if he went into a predominantly black neighborhood, he would be in danger because they would rightfully want revenge based on all the harm whites have caused. I asked him where he saw such acts of revenge that would lead him to feel that this really could happen. With all the overt acts of cruelty from burning churches, to hate crimes, to systemic violence whites have committed, when has he heard about random acts of revengeful violence by blacks. He thought about it and agreed that only rarely was this the case and that I was right. Yet, it is this false fear that often stops whites from entering melanated communities and making meaningful connections.

Many white people usually don't even consider the flip side of this story. When visiting Nelly's father at his home in the inner city of Saint Louis, he and some of his neighbors spoke about how scared they were to cross from the city limits into the county. They feared being watched. They feared being setup or framed for something they did not do. They feared being taken advantage of due to lack of knowledge or experience in situations that they had never encountered. Of course, they feared police harassment, brutality, or incarceration.

Melanated humans have to face these concerns on a daily basis for any of their needs that require them to move outside of their comfort zone. These fears are based on the realities that exist because of the systemic oppression that we have created. Low-melanated humans, though some of their fears may be valid in some circumstances, are not faced with the same reality if they take a chance to venture outside of their comfort zone. If by some chance white folks are victimized, they would have the full support of the system in place to rectify the situation.

Fear of making mistakes: In many of the conversations I've had in white antiracism groups, the comfort is in the protest, but the actual community development brings forth fear of making mistakes. "I don't want to say something wrong," "I don't want to come across as a white savior," I hear my fellow whites say. I respond, "You already have made mistakes and you're okay." The biggest mistake we make is not to do anything because of these fears. Now that we have all experienced this fear, hopefully, we can get past it, learn from mistakes, let go and learn how we can contribute and share space.

Jealousy and envy: I believe that a deeper fear is losing our identity as being superior. Perhaps, we are really afraid of how we will perform in a truly "merit-based" system. In an equal playing field with equal opportunities, where does that leave us? Given that our energy is often spent, not on focusing on our own abilities and greatness, but rather on positioning ourselves for power, when we find ourselves in the same circles as others, how do we perform in comparison?

As mentioned in the Step 1, racism is massive bullying. It stems from jealousy and envy. It's ironic, in a culture that focuses so much on individualism, how often we measure our success in comparison to others. Jealousy and envy are traits that we must let go of in order to experience a greater appreciation of the journey of experiencing life with other cultures.

My grandmother, Mimi, taught me that emotions swing on a pendulum. The more you care about something, the greater the swing when you lose it. In our institutions of learning and communications, we are taught that we are the moral leaders to the world, that we know what is best, which is why we are colonizing the rest of the world. We developed this inherent sense of pride in our superiority.

Too often, we are faced with the fact that it's a false sense of pride. This false sense of pride shows up in white nationalist groups as the desire to maintain our imagined superiority. On the other end of the spectrum, many progressive whites want constantly to oversee and direct the healing process. We feel this sense of responsibility to make a difference. But the real difference is in not leading. It's in healing our own minds, while at the same time supporting the transformation, and going through the process of letting go.

Overcoming peer pressure: When I was growing up and came to a crossroads in my life, my best friend's brother, Mike Jordan, often used to tell me, "Peer pressure is a mutha..." Being concerned with what those closest to us will think of us can have a deep influence on what we do. Many lo melanated folks who realize the need for change and truly desire to make a difference often find themselves facing becoming an outcast in their social circles. Being a change agent takes courage because of the pressure of our peers.

Joining organizations and support groups, such as WP4BL, can help alleviate some of this discomfort. It is often easier and more enjoyable when we are on one accord, rocking together if you may. Yet, because of this, we can slip into homeostasis and exclude ideas that are different. This happens often when groups are formed in any circumstances, even in antiracism circles.

I have often found myself on the outside because I do not share the same life experiences and perspectives as those who have found a home for themselves in this movement. Being different can feel lonely even though the movement's goal is all about celebrating those differences. It is important for us to remember to acknowledge, accept and even celebrate those differences as much as possible.

What brings about letting go

I ask myself a series of questions when I make real changes. What feelings do I have about speaking differently? What feelings do I have about behaving differently? What feelings do I have about interacting differently with the same people in my life? What can I do to let go of what I have been taught and let go of the fears about moving forward? What do we have to lose and what to gain? How can we reshape our approach?

For many of us, the courage to answer these questions sparks from some external event. Either we get a chance to see something that we didn't know existed that we want to be a part of, or we find ourselves facing a tragedy that makes us realize that we want something different. For some, it is a near death experience or life altering disease that helps us let go of what we valued. For some, it is the loss of a loved one that makes us realize that new values are needed to prevent a similar loss for ourselves or others.

The pandemic and the murders of George Floyd and Breanna Taylor shook the world with both of the latter happening at once. Now, we are having deeper conversations. The idea of change is the new peer pressure. If we want to outlast those who are against this transformation, we must let go of our past values and learn how to appreciate values of other cultures that we have previously been ignoring.

The challenge that so many of us face in changing our values is that they were instilled in us by our parents, family members, adults we looked up to, and peers at a young age. To want to replace our values may feel like we are saying that our parents and their parents were wrong. They guided and cared for us when we didn't know better. Given the value we placed on the positive interactions we have shared with the influencers in our lives, it is easy to be fearful of change, because change goes against what we've learned since birth.

Dr. Jason Plunkett was a member of my cohort in Phillips Graduate University. A black man whose family is from Belize, Jason was raised in Inglewood, California surrounded by gang life. When I met Jason, he was a practicing Marriage and Family Therapist who also worked for a juvenile detention facility focused on young sex offenders. Jason taught me about changing a person's mind through cognitive behavior therapy (CBT). CBT states that changing thoughts will alter behavior because our behavior follows our initial thoughts.

Jason explained to me that before we can transform our thoughts, we must change our values. Our values guide our perceptions. Our perceptions lead to our thoughts. Thoughts influence our feelings. Our feelings emote actions. Habitual actions become behavior. Habitual behavior develops into a personality and that persona becomes our character. Our values are given to us as we develop as children. As we are learning how to think and before we understand what is real or not, we form perceptions based on our values that, through the path Jason laid out, become our personality. The human brain is still developing well into our twenties and beyond, but we can form our personalities prior to the brain finishing developing.

Jason gave me a personal example. He said as a youth he was good with his hands when it came to fighting. This led to more opportunities to fight and showcase his skills. He became known for being a talented fighter. He valued his ability to win fights and it served him well, or so he thought, so much so that he accepted this attribute as his persona. Yet, he wanted to show people love. It wasn't until he was taught how he could alter his approach that he stopped pursuing his goal as a fighter. He started by making changes to his perceptions and thoughts.

For Jason to make that modification, he had to face his fears. Fighting got him a certain level of respect. Loving leaves him vulnerable to harm by those he opens up to. Yet, he also was inspired by the likelihood that he would not be harmed and that he too could receive love in return. That idea was enough to face his fears and shift his values. In that change process, he first had to let go of his perceptions of who he was and how life operates. This is where we are as a society. We want a better quality of life. We developed a perception that our war-like ways will provide our desired results.

We are going through the transformation process, which as Deepak Chopra said, can be chaotic. Some of us are trying to hold on to our condition and more of us are pushing for a different way of living. As we are deciding what we will become as a nation and a world, letting go of our old values and opening ourselves up to new ones is the chaos we are in right now. Ultimately, however, letting go has the greatest impact on all of the other steps. It is something we must learn and repeat throughout the process of change and throughout our lives.

Step 4

Appreciating the Value of Others

In any villain story, the captured are not allowed to know what's happening on the outside because knowing there's a hope of escape and survival motivates the captured to fight to get free. Awareness of alternative possibilities is the biggest threat to any type of oppression. In this instance, Black Power is not a threat to white supremacy culture because we fear what black humans might do to us in return after years of subjugation. Black Power is a threat because black power stands for creativity, truth, equity, togetherness and justice. And we whites are holding the world captive because we are too afraid to imagine what the world would look like without us running the show.

Creating white supremacy culture is hurtful to ourselves because to maintain it we must spend so much time and energy trying to suppress others rather than being our best selves. Untangling our harmful ways takes identifying them for what they are and freeing ourselves from this pattern. White culture thrives on deception, control, consumption and individualism. Maintaining this system of oppression also harms us because we are missing out on the contributions to society that melanated humans would be able to accomplish if they were allowed to be the best version of themselves. Liberating melanated humans promotes life and all things possible. Hopefully, this will bring the end to a death-based culture.

Step 4 is about continuing to uncover the tactics used to create and maintain white supremacy culture while acknowledging the greatness in others as well. We talked about the direct mission to design a system of harm and the tools used to create the image of superiority. Now we will examine how we see and experience others, in particular black culture. The ultimate goal of Step 4 is to have us gain comfort in appreciating the contributions and greatness of black culture without being threatened by doing so. This recognition will give us reason for correctional actions. It is imperative also to begin to shred some of the superiority complex and to practice humility. One of the ways to practice humility is to give credit to others where credit is due.

How we tell our stories

In January 2017, the film *Hidden Figures* was released. It's about three black women who provided the brains behind NASA's launch of astronaut John Glenn into orbit, an achievement that stunned the world. Learning about this movie, I immediately had mixed feelings. On one hand, I shared the pride in America's NASA operation - especially around the time of this story when the U.S. was fighting to be the first to orbit the planet and first to land on the moon. On the other hand, I was frustrated to have just now learned of this true tale of black women's brilliance and heroism at NASA. Shouldn't this story have been at the forefront of or, at least, woven into my U.S. history classes growing up? Shouldn't the names of these black women be synonymous with American patriotism?

Realizing just how hidden their contribution has been confirmed my suspicion of white supremacy culture. It has a long tradition of hiding the history of our relationships with and the contributions of aboriginal and indigenous humans. In Step 2, we revealed how we hid information of the harm we caused to black folks and the impact of slavery. In the case of Hidden Figures, we not only hid the great accomplishments of these black women, but we took credit for it.

Reversing this habit is a key factor to Step 4. Instead of keeping the contributions of others hidden, we must actively research, learn, appreciate and value the contributions of melanated humans and their culture, in this case, "black culture." As we do this, we must also recognize and acknowledge how we have treated characteristics and accomplishments we like from black culture and how we designed a system to portray a certain image of black culture.

A week before going to see the film, I met author Jordan Flaherty who wrote *No More Heroes,* through the organization White People 4 Black Lives. He told us, amongst other things, how Hollywood made a conscious effort to portray white heroes even when the story is about life in black culture or based on a true story of a black human. Studio execs still told the producers that if they make the lead actor white, the studios will produce their film.

With this bit of information fresh in my mind, I went with Chevela to see the film in a theater. Needless to say, the experience was eye opening. During one climactic scene, actress Taraji P. Henson's character gave a very impassioned speech after having returned from walking a half mile to use the restroom. She was not allowed to use the nearby restroom for white folks and had to once again pay the exhaustive black tax on foot. Kevin Costner's character was her boss and was upset as to why she was gone so long when he needed her to give him answers to a math problem.

The next scene showed Costner tearing down the bathroom signs and declaring that anyone can use any bathroom. The crowd in the theater, mostly white, erupted in cheers. Chevela and I looked at each other and shook our heads. All that I could think was 'they got their white hero.' No one cheered for Henson's speech. And it was her great response to his questioning that motivated his action.

He didn't make that modification until her oppression inconvenienced him, yet his action drew the cheers. Ahh, what prestige will do to us. I do not believe much thought went into the cheers and I am sure the reason for cheering was as much about the adjustment and progress as who did it, but the incident provided me with something to think about.

What we don't tell

Why was the *Hidden Figures* story chosen to portray the contributions of blacks? It appeared to me that this story was chosen because it portrayed black loyalty to our armed forces which is at the heart of our "American Pride." We created a movie that portrayed black women doing what they could to be a part of "our greatness." There were so many other choices that would have been great stories. Black humans led many medical breakthroughs. We benefit from heart surgery, a technique developed by Daniel Hale Williams, founder of America's first black hospital.

Black inventors created the traffic light, filament in our light bulbs, personal computers, gas masks, silicone retinas, furnaces, pacemakers, wooden clocks, and countless other devices we depend on every day. Yet, students who care to learn of these accomplishments too often must go above and beyond to find the truth of these accomplishments. Needless to say, we'd have far less national musical culture to boast of without black artists' influence. Nor would we possess the greatest capitalist economy in the world.

Enslaved and free blacks built the pioneering agricultural industry through which most powerful, white legacy institutions gained their wealth. Along with the Chinese They erected train routes across the country, designed and mapped out the city of D.C., built the White House, and fed and raised millions of white babies. There is hardly any industry that black people have not contributed to in significant ways. Yet, as whites, we often take credit for the success of their greatness. Let's humble ourselves and level up to recognize the value of melanated humans. Once we learn to appreciate and value the humanity and contributions of aboriginal and indigenous folks, our behavior towards them, ourselves and the planet hopefully will transform.

Recognizing the true value of enslaved Africans

Let's dig a little deeper into a couple of areas. First, let's talk about the history of laborers and ownership. It is not that we just forced some random group of people to be our slaves to build our wealth. We chose a certain people to do so. We did not teach them to farm, having had no experience of our own. We did not whip them as we taught them the proper way to manage the crops. We chose them because we knew that they were highly skilled agriculturists, crafts people, industrialists, scientists, healers, master caretakers, and much more.

In West Africa, from where we purchased them, their trade-based societies were highly advanced, boasting of currency, mastery of the land, architecture, government and intricate social order and religion. We simply did not have skills to match them. Instead, we used our skills to manipulate and force them into bondage to do what we were not confident to do ourselves. We could have asked for their help, learned from them and bettered ourselves. We still can, which is why this is so important.

Why did we want black women, who we portrayed as inferior for centuries, to raise our children? What did this signal and teach white children in the process? Since slavery and until recent years, black women and men have been exploited as domestic servants, from raising children to providing and caring for the home environment. Do we really place a lower value caring for our home and family? I think just the opposite. I think we know that they are valuable, and we feel inferior in our ability to connect with nurturing our most important treasures, our family and our homes. Yet, going back to our feelings of insecurity, we lash out and demean those whom we have delineated as inferior - as if they are forcing us to feel this way.

Look at the caretaker industry now, especially in the medical fields. Whites tend to be the management because we feel better suited to usurp capital from the real valuable members of the industry, those who actually care for others. Just think for a second that former Mississippi Governor George Wallace, as he became dependent on care, wanted black women to provide that care for him. One of the most belligerent racist leaders of the South, who admittedly behaved that way to win votes, in his ending days wanted to be cared for by the women who he spent his popular life belittling. When his life was coming to an end, he admitted that he was wrong. Does he deserve to be commended? HELL NO! But his story can be an eye opener for the rest of us.

Ben Ammi teaches that the Hebrew writings claim the servant as the most valuable asset in the Kingdom of God. This is a concept found in most religious and spiritual writings. There is no greater act of humanity than to serve each other. I encourage us to recognize the greatness of a people who took all of our abuse and continued to serve. As we look to appreciate the value of other cultures, we need not look any further than service providers, black, brown or white. They are just as valuable as anyone who is trained to make decisions of what costs to cut to create shareholder value. Yet, in a disconnected system, positions are rewarded significantly more than true value.

At the same time, we must be cautious not to measure someone's worth, or a group's worth, by their contributions alone. We need an even deeper understanding. Every person born under the sun regardless of their race and history deserves dignity and respect. That must be at the forefront of our social contract among one another. Only from a place of true respect for humanity can we grow and evolve as white people in a way that makes the world a better, more livable place. This is something we can learn from others.

Wait, God is black?

Let's also not get it twisted, black humans did not accept these acts of slavery and servitude because they were weak, and we were stronger. Melanated humans do not innately think like us. Imagine with all the damage and harm that we have done to black people, there are no signs of revenge – on the level of genocide – that ever took place in the 400 years since we first imported black people to America. Still to this day, the black-led human rights' quest (even among the more militant groups) is for equity and equality, not overcompensation and not for the pain and suffering of low-melanated humans. Aren't these the same values taught by religious leaders and texts worldwide?

That is a true sign of strength. Sure, feelings of revenge may be expressed when releasing anger from the pain they have endured, but expressing those emotions have proven to be a better way of dealing with the pain than suppressing and acting them out in other ways. In their own healing, let's recognize how black folks have always looked out for us.

From what I have experienced, they have considered the wellbeing of white folk due to our advantages from controlling the system. Yet, I also have witnessed how they watch out for us mostly because their natural sense of connection leads them to do so. They know more about us than we know about them. They know we have been raised to ignore others and they have still been our keepers, like parents who hope their children wake up some day to realize the errors of our ways.

If we are going to move into a healed society and world, then it is time to accept that our religions are created from stories of melanated people. The Hebrew writings were written by melanated humans for their society. Upon going through the Northeast African Regions, our Greco-Roman culture took these scriptures and added our own interpretations.

More importantly, all over Europe and spread through colonization, the paintings of these biblical figures became low-melanated and portrayed the Gods of these stories to look like the Greco-Roman Europeans. It is time to acknowledge that the messiahs of these stories and the humans that wrote them did not look like us. If we are truly in a post-racial society, then it should not alter how we feel about our religious scriptures and the lessons they provide. If we are being honest then our Gods are black and brown humans. Interestingly enough, Hollywood and advertisers already often demonstrate this imagery.

Look at how many times God is portrayed as black in film and television. Even the racist Archie Bunker in All in the Family, a sitcom from the 70s, has an episode where he is praying for God to show up and his black neighbor does. Then look at Nike, Coco-cola, and so many other companies that have used black athletes and entertainers to persuade the masses to purchase their products. It is only natural that black culture is often imitated.

This could be known as the biggest form of flattery. Except we have a problem giving praise to black folks and black culture. I think this ties into the fact that we have portrayed our Gods with white skin and that has supported our feelings of superiority. That is a tough pill to swallow if, for all this time, we would have to grapple with the fact that those who we oppress the most are the ones who truly represent the God-like presence.

Black lives are valuable

Through all the pain we have caused, the latest movement is called Black Lives Matter, not Black Lives Are Better, or Black Lives Are More Valuable. There is humility in this name. I understand that BLM is an imperfect organization and movement (but I challenge you to name one organization or movement that has been perfect). It is also an idea, the actual words black... lives... matter. From the organization standpoint, it means that there's a home in the struggle for those committed to racial justice. And there's a phrase that everybody can understand and start to identify with, whether you identify for or against it. There's something specific that you can identify when judging how you want to be involved in or against racial justice and equity.

As far as the actual saying itself, it doesn't go far enough for me. I say this from just the term itself. "We matter" is not enough. Rather, black lives are valuable, and they have always been valuable. Black culture is valuable. We know it because we see the influence of black culture. We see the power of it, and we use our power to define it as American. We don't acknowledge that we've identified black culture as American culture. As a next step in the racial justice movement, we must learn to acknowledge with love and affection the beauty of black culture. When we show appreciation, our thoughts ease around the changes that need to happen. The adjustments aren't so threatening or looked at solely as a cost, because we can see value there.

In the world of finance, which has been one of the vehicles we have used to control our advantage and grow the equity gap, the terms "appreciation" and "value" go hand in hand. Given our power to define, we have chosen to value assets owned by whites higher than assets owned by blacks. In doing so, we have appreciated those values. As we look to address our racism, appreciation for black culture and black humans is imperative. If we can learn to do so, our valuation will amend, and it must. In the process of reevaluation there is an opportunity to heal.

Say it loud

If Step 4 makes you squirm, that is a positive step towards change. Lean into it. It is okay to recognize the greatness in others without having to feel any different about yourself. During an interview on All the Smoke Podcast, hall of fame broadcaster Jim Gray spoke of the influence of Former US Olympian and documentary producer, Bud Greenspan. When asked about Gray's display of humility, Gray referred to when Grossman said, "I knew I was good when I could look at someone else's work and admire it." It's easier to recognize and value the greatness of others when we take the competitive spirit and zero-sum mentality out of it. Then we can focus on being the best versions of ourselves while supporting the same in others.

Sin LaSalle, a character played by Cedric the Entertainer in the film *Get Shorty,* addressed this conundrum, "…How is it that you can disrespect a man's ethnicity when you know we've influenced nearly every facet of white America, from our music to our style of dress, not to mention your basic imitation of our sense of cool – walk, talk, dress, mannerisms. We enrich your very existence, all the while contributing to the gross national product through our achievements in corporate America. It's these conceits that comfort me when I'm faced with the ignorant, cowardly, bitter and bigoted who have no talent, no guts. People like you who desecrate things they don't understand when the truth is you should say 'Thank you, man,' and go on about your way."

Let's take it one step further and say to black Americans, "On behalf of white people, I apologize for the harm done to you, your ancestors, and this world. I recognize and appreciate your contributions and the example you have set for us. I aim to repair the harm of our injustice."

Step 5

The Case for Reparations

"To be a slave. To be owned by another person, as a car, house, or table is owned. To live as a piece of property that could be sold—a child sold from its mother, a wife from her husband. To be considered not human, but a 'thing' that plowed the fields, cut the wood, cooked the food, nursed another's child: a 'thing' whose sole function was determined by the one who owned you. To be a slave. To know, despite the suffering and deprivation, that you were human, more human than he who said you were not human. To know joy, laughter, sorrow, and tears and yet be considered the equal of a table. To be a slave was to be a human being under conditions in which that humanity was denied. They were not slaves. They were people. Their condition was slavery." - Julius Lester, African American/Jewish writer

Economic and political reparations for black descendants of the Transatlantic Slave Trade are absolutely essential to the liberation of all Americans, and all people across this world. According to the Brookings Institute, reparations are a system of redress for egregious injustices. They are a form of atonement that is not foreign to the United States, which I will explain more later in this section. Yet, Black people have yet to receive systematic repair for the centuries of denial of wealth that slavery afforded white families and institutions, and for state-sponsored barbarity, genocide, Jim Crow, and Co-Intel Pro.

To refuse to give reparations for this type of treatment continues to deny black people their humanity, while at the same time denying white people the benefit of atonement. Embedded deep in the white psyche is the reality that the humans who were enslaved are the ones during that period who displayed true humanity. It is time that we repay such humans and ask them to not only forgive us but also to teach us how to practice such levels of humanity.

In his 1999 standup titled Bigger and Blacker, Chris Rock once proclaimed, "None of you would change places with me. And I'm rich!"

The great diversity educator Jane Elliot, most famous for her efforts using eye color to show the repercussions of racism, brought this same idea to an audience in a different manner. She was speaking to a crowd mostly of white folks: "I want every white person in this room who would be happy to be treated as this society in general treats our citizens, our black citizens, if you, as a white person, would be happy to receive the same treatment that our black citizens do in this society, please stand."

She repeated the question as if they must not have understood and no one stood either time. She claimed that it is obvious that we know what's happening to black folk and that we do not want that for ourselves. So why are we willing to let it happen to others? I believe that in the answer to Jane's question lies the reason for why we need reparations. I also believe that her demonstration proves that we all know this to be true.

My son Stephen, 16 years old at the time, joined me in a conversation with Audrey, my best friend from White People 4

Black Lives. He told us how he was explaining to a white friend the idea of reparations. His white friend was telling him that it was not right to take what is hers because she was not the one who did the damage. Stephen astutely made it personal. He said, "So if your grandparents wrongfully stole something from my grandparents and it was passed down two generations to you, doesn't that rightfully belong to me? You have what was supposed to be passed down to me." That's exactly the point, especially in a culture that we created where we are possessed with possessions.

Overcoming our excuses

Reparations has been difficult for white people to grasp because we talk about reparations solely from a slavery standpoint. We now fear that it is too late and too confusing. Some excuses are the cost is too great - as if we do not create our own money and value system - or we do not know who to give what to because of immigration and interracial relationships. Well, to address the second, I would say it is better to be mistaken by doing too much right than not enough. Think about that for one second.

That question comes from a scarcity mentality driven by fear and not connected to humanity. Why in our world are we more scared of doing too much good than not enough? We think it is a horrible crime for us to be taken advantage of that we would rather do less good than to let someone undeserving get a boost – but an undeserving boost is how whites got and stayed ahead since the early development of our country. There is obviously more than plenty to share if Bill Gates can be the largest farmland owner in the USA. He doesn't farm himself. He can afford to buy food. Why does he have so much control over our food? And we struggle with the idea of reparations. That's a system made from a disconnected mind.

We are far removed from American chattel slavery, yes. But I do not measure the need for reparations as such. The reality is reparations for southern slavery were decided upon and then reversed by U.S. President Andrew Jackson and his cronies. So the mandate to atone never happened. Yet, shortly after slavery was determined illegal, black folks were elected to prominent positions of government until they were systemically removed by voter suppression.

Then came Jim Crow, a wave of insidious laws and practices to limit black potential. During this time, segregation was weaponized. Then and still now, black communities built business districts such as Black Wall Street in Tulsa, Oklahoma that were either bombed, torched, or systemically forced into dilapidation. Then came the Federal Housing Administration and Veterans Affairs programs that were established for economic growth and the black folks were once again systemically left out. This was another huge growth spurt for white families to receive loans, home ownership and greater economic value and support.

As if that wasn't enough, we had the illegal actions of law enforcement through Co-Intel Pro to design the way we police our black communities today. Co-Intel Pro was the FBI and law enforcement's mission to stop black power organizations and stop the rise of a black Messiah and the ramifications carry on to this day. After this illegal conspiracy was exposed, rather than bring justice, the government ventured into a "war on crime." From the President Nixon era through today we have made imprisonment a big business, as destructive a display of how capitalism works as possible.

We have systematically targeted black human populated areas for dumping drugs, alcohol and firearms, replaced healthy food access with processed and fast food access, devalued their property arbitrarily, and targeted them for drug crimes, for which they were then punished by imprisonment with much stricter sentences than any other group, especially whites, for the same crimes.

We redlined them to live in areas where the pollution levels were worse, gave them less access to hospitals, and continue to treat them differently inside the hospitals. All together this has led to 13% of the U.S. population fighting over .5% of the wealth. If you think that reparations for slavery is too complicated this late in the game, I agree. We need reparations for much more than just slavery. We need reparations for the atrocities committed throughout the over 400 years of systemic intentional behavior to attempt to destroy a race of human beings who have been more vital to our wealth than we acknowledge.

We have the model for repair

Reparations are as American as apple pie. Just as racism is. Therefore, descendants of enslaved people and other natives who substantially built this country's wealth for us and suffered throughout our country's history by whites' targeted oppression have been denied access to reparations. We have given so many of our institutions "reparations" when policies and practices have hurt their business profits.

When persons are injured in accidents, when persons are forced to lose something or wrongfully have something taken from them, we give a form of reparations. Our legal system is designed to make persons whole when there are "damages." Our insurance system is in place to pay the costs of making whole what has been damage. We design subsidies and bailouts from our tax income. Subsidies do not repair, rather they give a foot up. Bailouts make up for losses caused by the entities themselves. We are comfortable with these forms of boosts and repair, but are uncomfortable with paying reparations for our intentional harm?

As my mentor, Dr. Robert Gordh, Philosophy PhD and Los Angeles activist, and I have discussed, a person crossing the street in the correct way yet being accidentally, severely injured by the fault of a driver has the opportunity to be repaired. The injured human lying in the street is helped up by paramedics into an ambulance and taken to a medical facility. Throughout this repair process, payments are covered for the losses due to the damages themselves, for medical services to repair the injury, for time for rest and recuperation, for therapy sessions for rehabilitation, and for lost wages.

The injured human is not told to get out of the way because they are blocking traffic or that he or she needs to let go of what just happened. Nor is the injured party told to pick themselves up by their bootstraps and get on with their life even though they cannot walk. We know that, if you do not properly treat a severe injury and you continue to use that part of your body, the injury will worsen. In order to compensate for the injury, other parts of your body will become misused and damaged.

Eventually this will take a toll on that human's health, mind and internal organs as that person will struggle to get needed exercise and adjust to not being as capable as before. This is why we do our best to compensate for injuries. Even after surgeries and rehab, one may never fully recover. At least they will get support in their attempt to be made whole. We need to take this approach in reparations for a community of humans that we have severely injured.

What about the cost?

The big concerning question I am often asked by whites is what is the cost? And that's not the right question if you're only going to stop there because we spend large sums of money all the time. That's what we're about. When we walk out of the door every day, our expectation is to spend some money, whether it's on gasoline to get us to where we need to go, or we're going to a store, or whatever it is, we're most likely going to spend money.

If we're spending money on our bills at home, we're not thinking only about the cost. We also think about what those bills provide us. Oh, they provide us electricity. They provide us water and gas. They provide us an ability to cook. They provide us a sense of comfort, protection, access to enjoyment and more. If the home becomes damaged, we look at all costs of repair and then consider how much we value what we will repair.

The cost of reparations must be considered along with the value. It's not just valuing black lives, but what does a life where we don't have a certain level of targeted poverty look like? What does experiencing life with other cultures really look like? And how valuable would that be to us? The problem with determining these answers is we have been taught not to know. As previously mentioned, we do not learn about the value of other cultures. On top of that, we have done our best to remove black people's understanding of their own culture from the time we enslaved them until present.

The most patriotic of us keep emphasizing that America is so great that everyone else wants to come here. Because we think we have what others want, we don't get to learn how to appreciate and value others. Thus, it becomes very difficult to have a conversation around reparations because now we're only seeing costs. We refuse to consider the value. That is why Step 4 is so important.

We know the value of electricity. We know the value of clothing and food and entertainment when we go outside. We know those values and we have no problem spending money for them. We might complain about the amount. But we know that there's value. We don't know the value of justice. We don't know the value of repair, but we could imagine what a community that has suffered from our intentional harm this long can do with the intentional support for growth and healing.

The bottom line is that so many other groups in America except blacks have gained from intentional support, such as subsidies and bailouts to farmers and corporations. Many of these entities have not suffered from harm. They simply get to benefit from the support. It is time that we see how the benefit of support for black human beings and communities will result from reparations.

Missed opportunities

Starting in the '40s and continuing through the '60s and still today, the FHA and VA lending opportunities were implemented to benefit whites only. While White communities increased their wealth, the opposite happened for black folks because they were left out of the chances to increase their wealth. Without opportunities to control resources, they watched their white counterparts gain tremendous stability and wealth in real estate as home loans made housing more valuable because payments were affordable. From the increase in value of real estate came investment opportunities, whether the home values were used for college tuition or to invest in businesses or more real estate. This further increased the gap in wealth between white and black.

Just as the FHA and VA loans were created with the potential to be an opportunity to help all Americans and could have easily been tweaked for reparative justice, we are currently missing the boat in two other key areas of growth. Marijuana and natural products industries have been growing fast, especially over the past ten years. Yet, because no intentional decisions were made for repair, the majority of the wealth is being generated by those who already had wealth to begin with.

These missed opportunities are truly disturbing because of how melanated humans have positively impacted the natural product space or how they were negatively impacted by the illegality of marijuana distribution. Let's take the cannabis industry. It is well documented and discussed that black folks were often severely punished for possession and distribution of marijuana and that this took a significant toll on the black community as a whole.

While intentional recourse has been made in an affirmative action manner, the results don't nearly repair the harm done. Sure, there is publicity around the number of black athletes in the cannabis space and there are programs for black and other minorities to get involved, but not in a position of control or with the same opportunities to gain wealth. The large corporate investors have the established wealth to control those positions. This newly formed industry was not designed to be used as a tool for reparations. The same white culture mind that developed this industry has ruled for far too long. Repair is not the priority. Wealth and control are.

The Natural Products Industry is even worse. We need natural products because of the products that were created and manufactured by white culture. The poisoning of our soil; the harmful additives, preservatives, and artificial colors and flavors; and the processes to mass-produce products are all results of colonialism. They are as white as suntan lotion. The pharmaceutical industry is based largely in Europe and fully colonized nations such as the United States. Therefore, we are the reason that there is a need to have a Natural Products Industry. Yet we control that industry as if it was our idea.

I have been going to the Natural Products Expo for several years. Each year it continues to grow exponentially. It is almost sickening to see how white it is, especially because I know that KOY soul vegetarian restaurants have been around since before vegan was a thing to consider. I see so many small natural enterprises created by black folks at the farmers' markets. To see similar products to those created by black folks mass-produced at a greater quantity without the same quality, saddens me greatly.

Unless and until we have intentional reparative justice, where we pay our debt to those we have harmed while they built colonizers' wealth, we will continue this plague. Until black folks can control their own supply chain and wealth generation, we are fooling ourselves, especially as we continue to cause harm to the planet and then capitalize on the repair to the damage we create. We are just continuing the cycle of harm. Reparations do not happen without the same level of intention that we have had to cause the harm in the first place.

White people need to heal too and a fast food fix won't do

Even if you believe the time is now for whites to mend and heal as well, we have to get away from the McDonald's approach that believes society will change overnight. This is going to take time and effort. It will not be conveniently delivered by Amazon to our doorstep. We all have healing to do, especially us white folks. Our desire for convenience and immediate gratification is causing us harm by conditioning us to lose appreciation for anything discomforting. We need to take the necessary time to look into why and what harm we are still causing for the pursuit of our own happiness. Hopefully, we can learn how to enjoy the journey once we are on it and finally heal ourselves of ignorance.

Let's say you are a basketball player and you have a severe injury. The severe injury causes you pain. The first thing you need to do in repairing that injury and pain is to stay away from further damaging it. You can't be told, "Hey, I know you just tore the ACL in your knee, but we need you tomorrow. So just get over it tonight. You got tonight and get over it and come on back tomorrow." No, you have physical pain, and you have to go through a process of healing.

We have to understand the process of healing all the pain society has created for so many lives. It is important to remain aware that we have never addressed the real understanding of why we've created such harm towards aboriginal and indigenous cultures. This is not just here in the USA but everywhere colonialism has done so much to destroy aboriginal and indigenous humans. We have to understand that the healing process not only takes time, but it is also going to be painful. We cannot run from that pain either. Back to the example, with this torn ligament in your knee, you need some sort of reparative action – surgery.

The intent of that surgery is to make a correction. This means that we must pay our large debt and give up control of assets and opportunities. Yet, when we make corrections, life teaches us that things get worse before getting better. In the case of the busted knee, you had to be cut open. Your muscles, ligaments, tissue and skin are going to have to heal. So now we've caused even some more harm in order to facilitate the healing process. We are capable enough to understand that as we make some modifications, it's going to possibly look worse before it looks better.

We created a level of hopelessness and inner fighting that doesn't just go away with money. And that's not on us to decide how the transformation goes. We have to get to the other side of what those modifications look like. We must also be aware that there's no one way to handle reparations. St. Louis healing will look different from Los Angeles. There'll be different kinds of healing from rural areas than from larger cities. Our role is to focus on the adjustments in our values, intentions and approach.

Next in the healing process on your knee comes rehabilitation through physical therapy. The physical therapy consists of cycles of pain and feeling better. The healing process will take intentional measures. You might need a pillow under your leg when you sleep or a brace and crutches to get around. The way you function during the recovery part of the healing process is not going to be the same as how you function in your life once healed. We have to keep that in perspective. For us to make the healing process work, there's going to be some painful conversations. There's going to be some discomfort in how we reallocate our resources. There's going to be uneasiness in these conversations and going into communities to help us all heal by learning about one another.

If we're really going to do that, we need to have a more desegregated approach and a more communal approach towards these things. How white folks show up in spaces occupied by black folks is going to bring various levels of anxiety for us. When invited, we need to learn as white folks to come into the black community in a way that is supportive of the black community. Instead of trying to say, "Well, I know best," or "Here's how I'll show up," try asking, "How can I best serve?" or "What can I do?" There have been times where healing from injuries have included setbacks. We might say something wrong or overstep what we have been asked to do and we have to understand that and learn from these experiences as well.

This may be true for others, as well. Everyone in this healing process is human and will likely make mistakes. It is a learning process for us all. When healing from pain, black folks may have many times where they still reflect on the pain and what could have been, or even why it took so long. They may not want to be bothered with us when we want to help. In our approach, we need to be aware of these possibilities. Healing does not mean act as if it never happened. We cannot expect there not to be scars or that we won't have lingering pain.

Using the leg injury example, the healed leg may never be like it was before the injury, but it still may be very functional. You still may be able to get out there on that basketball court, have a great time, perform, and be there for your team. As we go through the reparations process, we must maintain that desire and work through the issues that arise from the damage created over the last 400 years. If we know that our goal at the end of the day is to have a desired community, where we are sharing, interacting, respecting, loving and valuing each other, then going through the healing process doesn't seem so daunting. We can welcome some of that pain, knowing it will inevitably be better.

As I argue for reparations, I am not going to pitch an amount for it is not our responsibility to determine the value lost and what is needed to make it whole. Making the money available is only part of the repairing process. Determining how it will be shared, used and benefited on is not our role. Let's be clear, black folks do not need our help or guidance. We do not need to save them in this process. We are the ones who created the conditions that need repair. What right do we have to insert ourselves in anything that belongs to descendants of humans used as slaves and of indigenous humans of this land?

We are only responsible for letting go of our ideology that we deserve ownership. Ownership is about control. We need to give up the hoarding and get out of the way. We do not get to define reparations if we truly seek healing. The black community needs to be able to control its own access to the pillars of society, finance, education, land, food, healthcare, and communications. Otherwise, we will continue to use our economic system to maintain the imbalance and lack of resources. In our capitalistic system, it's a lot easier to gain further access to resources (to money, resources, opportunities, etc.) when you already have access.

The differences in the ability to access resources is something that too often white conservatives choose to ignore, while white liberals point out the problem to appear friendly but are not willing to make the intentional effort to correct the inequities. Malcom X pointed this out in his time and the same is true now. Malcom was very specific in his beliefs that no whites could be friends with the black community without defying the system.

I say we have enough proof that the systems we created are inhumane and, therefore, we do not need to challenge them, but rather create new ones. The mind of the destroyer need not lead the way. Rather, we must be open to the beautiful world that can be created when we step out of the way and let those who are better connected to the damage we have brought about, guide us.

Step 6

Being Led by a New Mind

"We cannot solve our problems with the same thinking we used when we created them." – *Albert Einstein*

While I have stated that the steps are not necessarily sequential and we will all go through different aspects of them from time to time during our journey, Step 6 and more so Step 7, are focused on the building process after repair in racial relations has been accomplished. The idea of the last two steps is replacing identified problems with new approaches. This is not to say that we cannot begin to humble ourselves and allow indigenous and aboriginal cultures lead us as we take the steps of repair.

Step 6 may help strike a balance when applied with the first five steps because we can use new leadership in our transformation process. We must also consciously remember that there are many people of color who have to go through their own healing and relearning before they can reincorporate the love and connection that we have taken from them. This transition from repair to learning a new modus operandi will continue to challenge our ability to work through discomfort, knowing that the end result will bring forth greater peace and well-being.

As we get deeper into the last two steps of the journey, assuming the first five steps generate real justice and equity, then the rebuilding will not focus on race in the same manner. As such, these last two steps are not as focused on race because the healing process of the first five steps would have brought a shift to how we value others. I am not suggesting that we pretend to be color blind, but rather we will be curious and respectful of different cultures and their values as we learn to reconnect.

These last two steps address some of the other harmful practices of our culture other than racism. A full description of the characteristics of our colonial culture that need to be addressed can be found in "The Characteristics of White Supremacy Culture" by Kenneth Jones and Tema Okun. Once we have identified the damaging traits of our culture and we have discovered a reason for showing greater appreciation for others, then we must learn to develop a new mind to help create additional improvements that we want to accomplish. As a white man, I cannot write what black folks would do when taking the lead in our relationships. Instead, I will share some comparisons of the Greco-Roman approach versus an Aboriginal/Indigenous approach.

What is a new mind?

As we support reparations for African Americans, a natural result of achieving repair is cultivating a new mind. A new mind means changing our intentions and approach to how we show up. As we learn to appreciate others and release our desire for control, we can allow different values to guide our thoughts and, subsequently, our interactions with one another.

I am not so arrogant that I believe that I have achieved the new state of mind. I am still reviewing my intentions and developing my approach. I am however deeply inspired by several experiences that have powerfully revealed to me the possibilities that could result from a different way of thinking. In March 2019, I attended a panel on "Prosecutorial Power in Transforming the Criminal Justice System." Two key speakers demonstrated to me the power of leading through a different approach to our justice system.

The first speaker was Adam Foss, former Assistant District Attorney in Boston, MA and founder of Prosecutor Impact, an agency providing training to help prosecutors make a positive impact in the community. Foss stated that the prosecutorial profession is ripe for reinvention and requires better incentives and more measurable metrics for success beyond simply, "cases won." He claimed that he experienced the "magic show" of deception as discussed in Step 2 when he attended an Ivy League law school before becoming a prosecutor.

He was taught about all facets of the law, such as real estate and corporate law that had nothing to do with criminal justice. Yet, he was taught nothing about sociology and how system design and social structure impact the community he would be "serving" by "protecting" them. Foss bemoaned the lopsided focus on determining punishment as opposed to gaining an understanding for what leads to "criminal behavior" in the first place.

I was most moved by Kim Gardner, St. Louis' first African American Circuit Attorney. Gardner is also a registered nurse and former state representative. She stood out for her approach to criminal justice reform. Gardner talked about her community outreach from her office. She requires that prosecutors in her office decide whether a person arrested is a threat to the safety of the community. If they are not, then her office will seek alternatives to incarceration. Essentially, Gardner transformed the focus of the prosecutor's role to rehabilitation and preventing the repetition of wrongful acts. She saw this approach as a better way to improve the quality of life and safety of the community.

After the event I introduced myself to Gardner. I told her about my work which, at the time, included working for a food justice organization. Much to my delight, she responded about her vision for her office to have a food bank. She said that if we can solve issues of those whose needs are not being met, then we will prevent much of the minor and desperate crimes that keep officers and her office busy. This is the type of new mind approach that leads to a more humane world. It broadens the boundaries of what a prosecutor's office can do to improve the life in the community she serves.

As I continued to hear Gardner speak in later engagements, I became more motivated to support her approach and vision. She cares about the community she serves, and the members of the community recognize her sincerity. At a later panel, I heard police captains talk about how involved she is in working with officers to modify the approach of policing to working as a part of the community. She leads with a vision of the police developing relationships with those they are committed to protect through service and building connections. Her vision for building a strong community is less focused on punishment and more focused on prevention. These are the transformations that protesters and activists are demanding in St. Louis and around the nation.

This is what the new mind is all about. It is not just about alternative police responses to a situation. It is a new approach. Rather than public servants focusing on crime and how to address punishment after it happens, we alter the intention to the officers' role to a more participatory one in the enhancement of the quality of life of their community. Inherently this approach will reduce the amount of crime through preventative measures, implying that crime under these new circumstances won't be considered so often as a viable option. Much of our resources will be used to build a better life rather than wasted in the destruction of communities.

Our challenge

In studying for my doctorate, I learned that one of the biggest challenges to the transformation process is the participants "not knowing what they don't know." This is a key factor in determining leadership's ability to recognize the need for change and guide the process. In applying that concept to antiracism work, I wonder can we recognize that as white folks, we often do not know what needs adjusting? If we have never experienced a world in which humanity thrives for all, then can we acknowledge that we may not know how to design such a world?

Incorporating a new mind is the most challenging part of the change process because it brings together all of the previous steps and adds the element of the unknown. The first two steps are designed to help us recognize that we do not know how to create a world that works for all and realize that we don't know what we don't know. Accepting a new mindset challenges our ability to let go. Learning a new approach means that we will have learned to appreciate the value of others enough to repair the harm. We have to develop methods to learn what we do not know and learn how melanated humans can educate us about how they see the world we both experience. We have to remain open to experiencing being guided through participating in new social structures.

One approach for a new way

As I have described, I learned about what a new mindset and approach may look like from the Kingdom of Yah. Their economic plan is interdependence within a community of shared values and resources. The KOY believes that universal laws must guide how we live, meaning that we must gain understanding of how life operates. It is our purpose to be a part of the flow of life. We do not have the right to create what Ben Ammi calls the "Imitation of Life," which implies that we shouldn't create our own rules that alter life on the planet. If something we create is harmful, then everything that comes from that will add to the harm or keep us from being connected to each other or to the world that we are a part of.

If we are genetically altering the foods that already exist, then not only are the effects from the alterations harmful, so will be the attempts to address those effects. Stop the harmful behavior and there is no need to address the negative effects. Otherwise, we get lost in a web of addressing one result after another further causing confusion and disconnecting us from the way the universe is designed to work. The essence of this connection and side effects is taught in some form in every religion or science. It is how we are taught to use this knowledge that creates the promised effect. Just because we can learn the order of the Universe with all its parts does not mean that we should choose to manipulate it in any way. I think the saying goes, "If it ain't broke, don't fix it."

From what I have learned about indigenous and aboriginal cultures, they do not practice these behaviors. The cultures that practice imitations of life are those who are the most mutated from our original human form. This may be the harshest pill to swallow, for those cultures are interested in dominating the world. But it doesn't have to be that way. The truth sets us free allowing us to open up to humbly improve and learn how to become one with nature. We can learn the benefits of being in harmony with the planet.

Other community ideas exist

Similar to the KOY is a non-profit organization called the Venus Project. It also champions the connection among all humans and our responsibility to the planet and all forms of life. Though still in the infancy stage, it has a different approach from our current social structures.

The Venus Project is self-described as an organization that "recognizes the important connection between global resource mismanagement and problems such as war, climate change, poverty, and hunger. In the broader context, these are all detrimental results of the current socio-economic operating system. In response to these challenges, this organization presents solutions through the holistic application of science and technology; two areas in which recent advancements hold the potential to make far-reaching positive impacts."

I first learned of the Venus Project from Jacque Fresco, one of the Venus Project's founding designers when he spoke about how we accept greed, jealousy, deceit, and other negative feelings as human nature and that is why we approach life by preparing our days to face others who feel this way. He noted that sharing, caring, supporting, and serving one another are also human nature. Since, our system is not designed with these values guiding our intentions, we do not practice them as a developed culture. The Venus Project approach challenges whether the world's present problems can be solved within the framework of today's social institutions.

Per its website, our current problems "cannot be solved politically or financially, because they are technical in nature," Fresco says. "We are at a time when transitional decisions should be considered that could permit us to evolve from our present culture of scarcity, waste, and environmental destruction to a caring society of ecological concern and abundance."

The Venus Project proposes to "redesign social institutions by applying the latest technologies 'to benefit everyone.' Members of the Venus Project contend that financial wealth is irrelevant to survival. 'The real value of any nation is its development and potential resources and the people who are working towards a more humane lifestyle and the elimination of scarcity. This can be accomplished through the intelligent application of science and technology.'"

Both the Venus Project and KOY are two of many new community styles in their early stages of development. It is important to recognize how long our current system of colonialism and racism have been in place when measuring the success of these newer communities. Hopefully, at some point this new way of living will find a tipping point creating a wave of new energy from future generations. Some of the ideas will be forced upon us by the damaging and inequitable results of our current approach demanding improvement. Younger generations who want to live differently than what we built for them may well foster this transformation and act through incorporating a new mind approach. They have greater access to learn about the value of other cultures and an understanding of how to use the technology being created.

How a new mind can work

Here are a couple examples of what an approach through the lens of a new mind looks like:

Technology has often been viewed as a threat or something that drives us apart. Yet, technology is our continued development of operational efficiency. To say that it in and of itself does something is a misconstrued point of view. Our intentions when using technology are what can drive us apart or connect us. If we use technology as an escape from dealing with one another then it becomes a wedge. The more we continue to substitute technology for human interaction, we will use it to remain disconnected. Technology also has the ability to bring us much closer together. We can share information easier. We can find new ideas for bringing us together. We can even travel faster to meet up.

The thought that we lose the ability to earn income because technology replaces us is also based on our approach. We could easily see it as beneficial that we do not have to put in the same hours of work to accomplish our tasks, if we saw the benefits of connecting with one another, rather than point fingers at how unproductive we are. Business owners are constantly looking to use technology to increase the speed of production and distribution. Yet, from what I've experienced, in facilities that maintain our current approach, using technology to increase speed is creating a high risk of personal injury and causing high turnover in the workforce. Hopefully this is a case of things getter worse until they get better. However, we can shift our intentions towards technology. As suggested by the Venus Project, we can make it available to all and use it to improve the lives of everyone.

Segregation is another example. We have been taught that segregation is inherently harmful and further divides us. We blame segregation for causing harm. Yet it is also a natural progression that occurs, whether it is in how we form communities or simply at social events. We tend to migrate to those we find similarities with. Who we interact with is fluid and can differ over time. We interact with different groups when we choose.

Segregation does not cause us to harm one another, but the way we have used segregation to keep us apart and for white folks to maintain dominance and to suppress others is damaging. How and what we are taught about others, far too often creates prejudgments rather than open curiosity. Because of a scarcity mentality we often approach other groups by looking at what we can take from them or them from us rather than considering what they can offer to us and us to them. We gain more from offering and receiving than from taking and deceiving because, in a world of abundance, which can be achieved by changing our economic system in ways such as is suggested by the Venus Project, we can meet everyone's needs.

What a new mind is not

There are many European led countries that demonstrate levels of connection and caring for one another. Michael Moore illustrates this in his film *Where to Invade Next*. He examined practices in European countries to demonstrate how much better they treat their citizens in comparison to the US in an effort to show how we can do the same. However, I was disappointed with his approach and, therefore, his conclusion.

Moore showed how Italian companies required employees to work less time on a daily basis and granted more yearly vacation than we do in the States. He showed how France prepares healthy meals for its students. He showed how Finland focuses its education system on social development and allows the students to learn together without pressure of homework. The results are that Finland has one of the top ranked education systems. Moore introduced countries with humane prison environments and free colleges.

No matter where he went, white folks treated themselves with respect and dignity, displaying levels of humanity. Yet, European countries have a history of colonizing other countries They do not behave the same in other countries populated by melanated folks as they do amongst their own. That is not by accident.

These countries do not tell the U.S. that we should correct our ways. They benefit from the US military force bullying the rest of the world. We are capable of being humane. But we choose to practice some levels of humanity only amongst our own populations while dominating other places to serve our lifestyle. In the same vein, it is our willingness to destroy others that makes us willing to destroy the planet and therefore ourselves. Moore could have exposed how melanated cultures also demonstrate progressive ideals that the U.S. could learn from. But he only showed European culture.

I don't mean to say that only white folks have been exploitative. The Hebrews and other Africans were enslaved throughout Africa by other melanated groups of people. To this day there are melanated people who demonstrate those same attributes and desires to dominate others. As I mentioned earlier in Step 6, I am not suggesting that we follow the practices of anyone simply because they have darker skin. Jones and Okun astutely pointed out in "The Characteristics of White Supremacy Culture," that there are many people of color that participate in white supremacy culture's ways. Still, European Greco-Roman culture is the prevailing culture that developed white supremacy culture. We must focus our efforts to modify this predominant culture in a way that eliminates the idea of one culture being inherently superior to another.

Of course, all indigenous cultures are not the same. There are, however, many ethnic groups with foundational values of connection that we should emulate moving forward towards the world we want to have. Just as the Greco-Roman Empire studied other cultures to learn ways to dominate and rule, we can learn from other cultures how to reconnect, share and support. I only wish Michael Moore would have begun his work by examining indigenous cultures of the world who colonizers have tried to damage and or eliminate.

Canceling each other does not help

I choose to define cancel culture here as implying that someone or company should not be available for commercial use because another group does not like it or disagrees with their perspective or point of view. This is a multi-layered discussion. The solution is not as simple as right or wrong.

On one hand, there are real situations that need to be stopped because of the harm caused to the environment and/or the harm caused to human beings' safety and ability to live their life. In some of these instances the people in position to stop the harm have either been a part of causing harm or had personal reasons for allowing the harm to continue for far too long. For example, the Penn State (Jerry Sandusky) and Michigan State (Larry Nassar) molestation cases affected so many children and their families. They should have been stopped much sooner. This type of moral canceling is needed. It is usually agreed upon among most people when what is stopped is horrible in nature.

On the other hand, cancel culture is very much a part of white culture. Among the many ways we use it, we do so physically and tangibly with our gun violence. There isn't a more absolute form of canceling someone than to kill him in order to remove him from our presence. Our history of overt racism employed by the white nationalist mindset is just that. In a less physical form, we are now trying to cancel each other's ability to speak. It's happening on both extremes of the political spectrum. On the right, athletes are told to "shut up and dribble," or, in other words, to stick to their profession and not use their platform to discuss social issues. Progressives also use cancel culture in ways to remove people from their position of influence based on previous actions or language that they disagree with.

Acts of disagreement and expression of views, even if they are racist, do not necessarily warrant having them lose their platform. There is a difference between a white nationalist calling for harmful actions in order to take back the country and someone like Rosanne who made hurtful comments that had racial biases. In this situation, Rosanne – through education and awareness – could learn from her mistakes and become an example of personal transformation. Imagine the numbers of people she could influence.

I do not see how we create progress if we do not work through these issues with real discussion, which may allow for some very uncomfortable and politically incorrect conversations to take place. Pretending a problem doesn't exist doesn't make it go away. Just because we're not looking at it doesn't mean it's not still there. I will give two examples of how this can be effective.

When Virginia Governor Ralph Northam was found to have worn blackface in his past, there were many who wanted him removed from office. Letting him stay in office, however, provided an opportunity to have him learn how to impact changes towards a healing process. According to the Washington Post reporting as he left office, Governor Northam gained valuable insight which he has demonstrated in the way he speaks about race. He made changes in policies around voting rights, criminal justice, and marijuana that positively impacted black communities. There is still work to be done to create equity, but would bringing in someone new have brought the same opportunity for growth?

According to polls from that time, it seemed as if a greater percentage of white folks wanted him removed, whereas a greater number of black folks who were polled wanted him to remain in office. I believe this reflects a greater understanding of how we can be most effective by allowing those who we harmed determine what is best for them in the healing process. Northam was in a position of power and influence. Although the conversations may have been uncomfortable for all, it would have been a missed opportunity for impactful healing to take place.

The second example occurred when Michael Vick, a former professional quarterback from the National Football League, was incarcerated for the mistreatment of dogs on his property. Vick served close to two years in jail and many animal rights organizations and protesters wanted him ostracized and never allowed to play professional football again. Yet, The Humane Society saw an opportunity to have Vick demonstrate that he had learned from his mistakes.

He became a spokesperson for the proper treatment and care for animals, specifically dogs. He remained in the spotlight and brought greater attention to the care of pets in a positive light. This was a much more effective way to have Michael Vick use his star power. As opposed to shutting him down as a form of strict punishment, Vick was able to demonstrate his humanity as a member of our society. We gain much more from working through the healing process than just the elimination of a problem or mistake or the person who makes the mistake.

I do not think we can heal without pain and discomfort. I also believe that it is more dangerous not to know that people with destructive feelings exist rather than having them out in the open for a heated debate. I want to emphasize the importance of making a distinction between opposition and difference. Not all change is about opposing values or completely stopping a value by canceling it as if it has no place.

It is not either or. Context is important. Opposition and cancel culture are like the two sides of the same coin. The two sides may differ, but that doesn't take into consideration that there are also different coins, or different ways to approach various scenarios. With a different approach, something other than direct opposition or cancel culture, we gain the opportunity to let a new mind lead us through the correction.

Re-defining winning

In the process of healing our mind, we should consider redefining our values of winning and competition, especially here in America. Our approach to making so many aspects of our society competitive is derived from the zero-sum approach stemming from the scarcity mentality. As I pointed out in Step 1, the idea of winning control led us to create the construct of races of people. There are many levels to how winning impacts our thinking. We have developed a win at all cost strategy, which is problematic.

This strategy becomes especially harmful in contexts where the methods of creating profits involve destroying life on the planet. Destroying life takes many forms, from low wages and exploitation of human beings to the poisoning of the environment. There are many written works on these various examples of destruction of life, which all relate back to the definition of winning that we use to justify the destruction.

In life, we create competition where it is not needed. Not all aspects of life are a game. We do not need to compete, for example, in serving one another or in creating and supplying items of need and comfort. Can we not see others in the same industry as participants and share revenue streams? Why do we need to see them as competitors? Yet, when people write a business plan, how they identify competition and what they plan to do about it helps determine whether they are investment worthy.

In the original idea of our free market system, competition was not seen as such a threat that we needed to destroy or acquire in order to get ahead. There was much more room for the allowance of many competitors. In this vision, the marketplace would allow for many to live comfortable lives. However, our culture did not allow this strategy to benefit the lives of many in this way. Instead of many sharing in the pie, domination by means of large corporations destroying small businesses has become the norm.

We make the medium of exchange part of the game of our society. The stock market and financial markets are ways to create wealth without actual value being created. Our money is becoming more and more abstract, and trading has become complex betting rather than true investing. Too many facets of this world are governed by the white supremacy culture mindset of winning and individual gain. Because of the winning culture, who's got "game" is important. As a result, in many of our systems one has to play the game, or she will be played. She will have to win at all costs or face loss.

I am curious in these "games of life," what are we winning? What have we defined winning to look like? We are taught to see others' existence as competition. How can we possibly bring forth a world that is compassionate and realize our connection to one another if our approach is to see others as competition first? Take entertainment and art, where does competition fit into artistic creativity?

We have been taught to believe that competition brings out the best in us. However, in most circumstances quite the opposite is true. So many great ideas and products never come to fruition, because the creators do not have the means to compete without their creations being taken from them or destroyed by the competitors. I do not see how this inspires us to be our best version of ourselves or to produce what is most beneficial.

Just because there are some circumstances that competition in sports can make athletes want to be the best version of themselves in that sport does not mean that it works in every facet of our life. Nor does it mean that it doesn't come without a greater cost than benefit. In the most recent Olympics, there were quite a few news stories covering mental wellness concerns among athletes because of all of the pressure put on them from external sources, be it fans, media, corporate sponsors, etc.

Furthermore, we colonizers compete for the earth's natural resources. How egotistical is that? If the resources are part of the earth that provides for us, then they should be shared, not competed over for consumption and control. A different mind can help us create an approach to work, community, and creativity without destructive competition.

Winning is so engrained in our culture that if we conjured a trick to deceive another human or group and we end up winning, based on our definition, does that somehow make us better than those who we deemed our opposition? Does that win justify the means we use to achieve the victory? Sadly, the answer in our society is far too often yes.

Think about how hollow we are that the result being favorable to a victor is more important to that victorious individual, group, team or nation, than the actual journey – the method and who was trodden upon – to get there. Winning is so ingrained in our culture, and it is done with too little value being placed on the road to getting there or sharing the fruits of what we can create.

Competition has its place

Don't get me wrong, I like a good competitive card or board game or sport. I am all for trash talking and backing it up. I am also for great sportsmanship because win or lose, it should not alter how we value each other and ourselves. It is a game. Yet we have become so entrenched in winning, how we examine sports has become so all or nothing. In professional sports we now measure the greatness of the athletes based on if they win championships.

Only one team can win in each league in each season. Does that mean that we cannot enjoy the competition and entertainment value that all other teams and players bring? These are great athletes, yet, because some of them do not win championships, does that take away from their greatness? Can we no longer appreciate the way in which they play because they haven't won the whole thing? In the media and on social media platforms, we judge so much about them based on championships.

I am not advocating for swaying to the other end of the spectrum, where we don't keep track of the score and every player on every team gets a trophy for participating. Eliminating competitiveness does not solve the issue. It is a competition and I say put your best effort to win. Enjoy the journey more than the destination and value what you can learn from it. At the end of the game or competition, we should all be able to appreciate the game for what it was and enjoy each other in the context of our life outside of the game.

Our obsession with sports

A professional athlete is still a human being beyond who he is as an athlete. Athletes also have a different perspective, as do most famous people because they get to experience lay people thinking they know them. Because of the limelight, they have the opportunity to be the voice of a new approach. For example, Russell Westbrook is an all-time, great athlete and NBA basketball player. He is considered by most as a ferocious competitor on the court who has yet to win an NBA championship. He was asked at a Washington DC press conference about his legacy in the context of winning championships. His response, "There is only one champion every year… My legacy is about how many people I can influence both on and off the court." As fierce as he is on the court, that's where it ends.

As a human, there is so much more to him than his competitive spirit and skills on the court. He takes great pride in his work in the community, fighting for justice by empowering others through education and through creating more and better opportunities. He holds true to his values, in which he prioritizes his family and friendships, and his interests in fashion. Wouldn't it benefit those of us who are basketball fans, to appreciate all of what he does rather than to find ways to put him down because the teams he played with did not win it all?

As we seek to transform our culture, how can we learn how to enjoy the spirit of the competition in the context of the games themselves? Can we learn to let go of the connection to the results after they are over? I am not saying this will be easy. I was once caught up in being a fanatic of the St. Louis Cardinals baseball team. I was in the Bahamas for a close friend's wedding when the Cardinals lost a close game in the playoffs. I was so upset I did not want to leave the hotel room.

Tracee, my date at the time, got so upset at how unbelievable my behavior was, I finally was able to shake it off and go out. I realized at that moment that I had a serious issue that needed to be addressed and I needed to let go of that result. It took me a few more minutes to calm down. I eventually left the hotel room and enjoyed the rest of the evening. But had she not called me out for how foolish I was acting, I may have missed a night that few have the opportunity to experience. More importantly, without being forced to reckon with my behavior, how long would I have continued to react that way or worse?

The system as a whole must change not just its parts

All parts of a system effect and are affected by all other parts. If we eliminate the police as we know it and do not modify anything else about our system, then we are most likely going to have an unsafe living environment. Yet, if we approach interacting in our community in ways that allow us to know and support each other, we can build trust. We can learn how to rely on each other to help us achieve our goals, work together to provide what's best for one another, and resolve conflict in a productive manner that prevents harm. Only then can we redesign public service to replace a significant part of policing because we will have methods in place to help us prevent or work through our disputes without police intervention.

We are in the midst of our transformation process as a country. The danger is allowing the same mind that built these systems to lead the process, which results in those in power staying in positions of power and privilege. Changing within the current social system is challenging because culture consists of habitual practices. If the core values of our social system do not transform, then the culture will revert to its same ways of operating with a different façade to appear as if modifications has taken place. If that happens, changes won't bring forth better results for us and for the rest of the world. As we let go, a new mindset led by a different set of values will better serve all of us and our leaders.

For instance, one of the hot topics in our mainstream media and corporate messaging is related to climate change. I am concerned that with all this talk, colonizers are still the ones leading the way for this action because of our economic position of power and media influence. How can Bill Gates, other international corporate leaders, and European national leaders think that we deserve to be the ones in charge of fixing a problem that we created? I do not hear white leadership sound humble enough to say that we are the reason our environmental concerns are happening. The language that I hear about plans of action are still based in economics and policies of the same systems that currently exist. They do not speak of changing how we approach our climate and what we must do to be a part of the planetary healing.

Connecting with the planet needs to be our goal. Even in the more progressive mainstream media and corporate messaging, I do not hear about how we must reconnect with the life the planet provides us. Outside of environmental advocate spaces, I do not hear discussions about the elements of the earth which can return us back to health. We could revisit the information we are taught in our primary education about the value of the nutrients of the soil, the air quality that trees and plant life provide, the quality of mental health that we get from connecting with the earth.

I witnessed these lessons in elementary school books when I was a substitute teacher. Yet we do not practice any of these teachings. Instead, they are used to test students. Lifestyle outside of the classroom does not reflect this understanding. By connecting with the natural ways that the earth and universe provide us with continuous life, we will better understand why and how to care for the planet that cares for us.

When I hear messaging about improving the environment, it tends to be hollow. Corporations use this conversational trend for marketing and not for true purposeful calls to action. In fact, corporate-led decision-making prioritizes profits over other aspects of life. Caring for the planet by repairing and preventing harm is counterproductive to our current cultural, profit driven, approach to life. As in any cycle of life, our approach leads to thoughts and actions that will continue to expand our disconnection with the earth.

Our values of individualism, winning, deception, and control all stem from the God complex that keeps us from understanding creative energy that exists. We need to reconnect to the rhythms of the earth's vibrations. Our decisions have removed us from understanding that these vibrations exist. A connected mind of indigenous cultures who practice behaviors that bring us together will connect us to the healing qualities that the earth provides.

Creating better racial relationships is the first step towards seeing the value in the benefits of other approaches. When we can value each other, our decisions will inherently strengthen our connections to one another. As the connections strengthen, we will see the errors of our past more clearly. On my journey, developing relationships with people from other cultures has given me the opportunity to learn from my mistakes. As the value we place on other cultures increases, it will be easier to allow others to provide guidance without feeling belittled or to provide valuable ideas to incorporate into our joint culture.

Servitude is our greatest value

In writing Step 6, my intensions were to introduce some possible concepts of what a new mind could look like. Surely, there are other ideas, concepts or practices that I have not mentioned that are applicable to this process. Defining and developing a new mind to lead us to a better future is a fluid process, not limited to boundaries that can be controlled and manipulated. Control and manipulation defeat the purpose of the new mind.

As low-melanated humans who have helped create our social structures that bring no sense of peace, moving forward through the change process, as servants rather than leaders, will help us become the best version of ourselves. Whereas white culture has promoted individualism, which values positioning for power and privilege, serving is rooted in the need for a "village to raise a child" approach that is common in aboriginal culture. There is tremendous value in serving others. We can serve by supporting those who have been oppressed by racism and colonization after we work through the reparations process.

These aboriginal humans demonstrate a desire for peace and justice rather than acts of blind revenge against those who look like the oppressor. They contribute to and influence our culture, art, science, infrastructure, nutritional wellbeing, and social behaviors while being denied credit for doing so. They have overcome much of the intentional harm that we have initiated, yet still serve and protect us in ways that we are learning to appreciate and may not fully understand. They definitely should be valued more greatly, appreciated, and celebrated as should all those who continue to practice these attributes.

If we learn to value how people of color have overcome our oppression and discrimination, we can move past our desire for denial. Rather, we can value what the opportunity to serve can teach us. Supporting those who continue to demonstrate such virtues, will help us develop new opportunities of living in a connected world.

Step 7

Manifesting Our Humanity

After achieving reparations, establishing a new life led by a new mind can create a humane lifestyle. In this type of society, the construct of race will no longer have a place. We humans (no longer defined by race) will honor, value and respect each other's culture, practices, and traditions and learn from one other. The result of the internal and outer work will be this final step - reclaiming humanity.

Step 7 is about the potential to redesign a world based on living responsibly and being connected to one another and to the planet. It is a working journey that we all will partake in together. It is not my place to dictate what humanity looks like moving forward once we have gone through the healing process. Rather, I am sharing how some of my life experiences have opened me up to the possibilities of living a humanitarian lifestyle. I'll touch on just a few of the possibilities that excite me the most.

The new mind from Step 6 leads to greater humanity and helps guide participation in larger community activities. It will be up to all of us – with our new values, new vision, new mission and new goals – to create results in addressing systemic transformations and creating a different reality. Ultimately, I am hopeful about the power of each of us to bring ideas to this healing and rebuilding process.

For example, in his hit song Nellyville, my beloved childhood friend Nelly painted a unique picture of this better world - starting with big cars and diamonds for every boy and girl in the hood. Although the focus is materialistic, within the lyrics lies a valuable vision of sharing and enjoying a better quality of life. I think ideas like these are a great starting point. Nelly goes on to share a vision of how we make decisions and eliminate problems that we can avoid. Nelly raps:

> Welcome to Nellyville, where all newborns get a half-a-mill'
> Sons, get Sedan DeVilles, soon as they can reach the wheel
> And daughters, get diamonds the size of their age - I'm talkin'
> One year get one carat, two years get two carats
> Three years get three carats, and so on into marriage
> Nobody livin average, e'rybody jang-a-lang
> Nobody livin savage, e'rybody got change
> Even the paperboy delivers out the back of a Range
> It's not a game it's a beautiful thang
> Imagine blocks and blocks of no cocaine
> Blocks with no gun play
> Ain't nobody shot so ain't no news that day...

The ambition and joy in this song is something I hope we take to this last step. When it comes to reclaiming humanity, we are more than capable. There's no limit to our creativity with Step 7. Through practice, learning from our mistakes and developing new ways, we will create a non-racist, life-enhancing culture. As we go forth, the beauty of living in a world designed to promote life will bring forth greater levels of interaction and functionality that we are not yet able to know is possible.

Enjoying the journey

One of my favorite sayings is "Perfection is a journey, not a destination." It is important to embrace the journey as we reimagine and realize our humanity. It's about learning, overcoming, and enjoying the multi-step process. We must work at it as if perfecting our favorite recipe, adding a bit of this, cutting away a bit of that, until the taste, flavor and texture are just right. We must continue to do this until it becomes second nature.

Most importantly, along this journey are infinite opportunities for improving ourselves and returning to our humanity. We must never feel limited in our quest for a better world. There truly is meaning and possibility in all the ideas we bring to the table. Now, as I reach the end of this book, what excites me the most is the possibility to reclaim the power to redefine our reality, to live in truth, and to nurture our innate need for family, community and love.

From deception to truth

Ben Ammi taught that our new humanity must be grounded in truth. Truth has the power of life. While lies break us apart, the truth builds stronger bonds. "Truth has the inherent power to produce the promised effect," Ben Ammi teaches. In other words, no matter how much we try to control outcomes, the truth will bring forth the real result. When we acted like we cared about ending racism after George Floyd was murdered and talked about the differences we intended to make, the truth will eventually reveal itself whether we truly mean what we say or just want to sound good and make black folks feel better about us.

Our current culture is built on the premise of lies and deception. No matter how we spin any conversation, we cannot hide the truth in its entirety. Therefore, we will see and feel the results of the truth coming to light eventually. Our choices to design a system to control and consume resources, both materialistic and natural, we result in destroying life as we achieve our mission. We say that our food science is doing wonders for the planet and humans on it, yet we use our science to create food-like substances that lead us on a path towards long-term medication and disease. This the result of an injured mind.

Our connection can be found in embracing that there are universal laws that govern the planet. We as humans do not have to redesign what already exists. The earth provides us the nutrients we need because we are made from the elements that exist in the earth. This relationship to the earth is simple and provides life. Gravity is a universal law that exists beyond our control, and we have accepted it and learned to live with it to the point that we do not think about it even though we connect with it. We can do so with other natural processes. As we remain curious, we must seek truth by questioning the effects of our actions on humanity and on the planet. As we share with and serve one another, we must be grounded in our connection.

Family is the foundation

Family, however structured, is the foundation of any community and society. If we live in connection with one another, it is easier and more efficient to make moves that are helpful and productive as a community. If we are functioning from a broken, disconnected state, pivoting as a community to make improvements in our culture takes more time and effort because we must first come together and learn to trust one another in order to make lasting transformation. If we have a bond of trust within the family to build upon then forming trusting relationships with others outside of the family is easier because the foundation exists. Inherent in this approach is demonstrating thoughtfulness, caring and support for one another. A society with this approach will reduce, and to the best of our ability, remove stress.

In the current society that we created, the powers to be have made, and continue to make, efforts to dismantle the family structure. From subliminal messaging in our entertainment promoting independence and dissent to the designed outcomes of our court system in family and criminal law, a broken home has become too much of the norm. Breaking from this norm is a challenge for us as we look to make a difference. Here, I am attempting to demonstrate how a shift in one aspect of our approach can lead to strengthening our society because all things are connected.

One of the most overlooked attacks on the family is the lack of support women have in breastfeeding their newborns. Breastfeeding is a process that is naturally best for newborns and infants to receive the nutrients they need. It is the initial foundation for a healthy mind, body, and spirit. The importance of breastfeeding should be taught so that there will be a widespread understanding. Our system of "health care" should be designed to support breastfeeding as much as possible. Our society should be structured to make sure our mothers are able to breastfeed for over one year without obstacles because we care about the wellbeing of our children. I use this as an example because we do not put much thought into something that is so essential: how a human life is initially nourished.

Currently, from the moment our children are born in the hospital to daycare, our children are whisked away into the system, removing them from the natural process of nursing. As soon as a baby is born, the nurses take the baby from the mother's arms to begin the "health care" process without even allowing a few minutes for baby and mother to take a breath, relax, and bond.

Due to the demands of our jobs and the lack of support to have women attend work with their babies present, we must find others who are paid to provide "care" for children. We fail to provide mothers comprehensive financial and emotional support during their most vulnerable time, forcing them to abandon one of the greatest emotional and health investments they can make with their child. As our children grow, they often spend more time with other adults and or in front of technology and media sources than learning the value of developing relationships with their family members.

The solution starts with changing our approach to one where we raise our children in a nurturing community. If health and wellness are essential values of a strong community, then our approach to birthing and raising our children will focus heavily on what is best for their health and wellbeing, starting with providing mothers with healthy food options knowing they are eating for their baby as well. We would make healthy food easily accessible. We would want the mother to be comfortable with minimal stress knowing that her body is going through so many changes. There are many aspects to consider when designing our communities to support such a goal. The intentions and benefits of the system design will impact everyone involved and extend beyond the mothers and newborns.

In the U.S., it takes far too much work and privilege to be able to actively participate in the process of building a family bond and raising our children. Ultimately, the bullseye of this targeted effort to dismantle the family bond has been the black family dating back to slavery. Ever since, our society has gone out of its way to influence a weak family and community structure and it's time for that to be repaired. Imagine how we can design a system that supports us as parents taking a more active role in guiding the development of our children. Imagine how neighbors can share in supporting us and vice versa. This is a basic principle of the "village to raise a child" approach that I learned about during my trips to Israel.

Redefining the value of our work

In a humanitarian world, we will value our dependence on one another. There are billions of humans on the planet. What makes us think that we are meant to be independent of each other, which is an absolutely impossible goal in the first place? We must depend on others to meet our basic needs. The idea of independence is that we work and can afford not to rely on others for money or other forms of support. Yet, there is no such thing. If you are an employer, you rely on employees. If you have a job you rely on those you work with and for. We rely on customers, suppliers, distributors, and so on.

In a humane society, work would be redefined to consider what is needed and what value it brings to the humans involved. We currently spend a lot of time worrying about how little the younger generations want to work. If we want a stronger family by allowing parents to focus on spending time with their family, how will we get any work done? Well, how much work is actually productive (meaning beneficial for ourselves, our society, and our planet) anyway? And aren't we all tired of the slippery slope of disconnection – from our families, from each other, from natural laws, and from productivity – that our current work culture entails?

In our disconnected world that prioritizes accumulating and controlling capital, we invest billions of dollars in research at colleges and corporations in creating an imitation of life. Back to the topic of breast-feeding, we have chemists designing fake milk products to replace breastfeeding. Why is this even necessary? While some women are not able to breastfeed, we are mainly doing this because we must be at work all the time and still struggle in so many ways, financially, emotionally, and or mentally. Instead of fake milk, we can put more funding into milk banks for those who need them.

With this huge investment in fake milk products, those who invested must now make a return on that investment, so they create marketing campaigns and influence healthcare providers to talk about the benefits of fake milk. We tout our science as being groundbreaking and fail to educate our children about the value of a mother's milk and the time spent bonding with the baby, which is crucial for brain development.

In the same disconnected world, do you know how much of our farmland that could be used to grow nutritious food that the earth provides us is instead used to create feed for the meat and dairy industry? According to research by the University of Oxford, half of the world's habitable land is used for agriculture. More than three-quarters of this is used for livestock production, despite meat and dairy making up a much smaller share of the world's protein and calorie supply. Even those who desire to continue to eat meat, should have more nutritious, fresh options instead of that which is mass produced for consumption. If we truly cared about our health, then most of the current crops would be drastically reduced. We would use only what we need to provide an abundance of healthy food.

To get us to appreciate our unhealthy diet, corporations driven by profits try to convince us that healthy living is uncool and unenjoyable. Imagine the amount of effort that went into making so many of us react to healthy living as if it is a negative constraint on our freedoms of choice. Great effort goes into creating this frame of mind. Great effort is needed to correct and heal from it. I could make this discussion into an entire book. But my point is that a simple shift in valuing the family by focusing on health and well-being beginning at childbirth means that we would have to design a system that supports our humanity. So much of the harm to ourselves and our planet can be eliminated by this simple shift in focus.

This one example demonstrates how a simple adjustment in approach to one aspect of the system affects all other parts of our life. The solution obviously entails more than what I have summarized and takes work untangling what we have been taught to think and feel in order to envision health and wellness making sense. I believe that we would enjoy the work of creating and implementing a system based on building bonds, supporting family structure and even supporting breast feeding mothers and our children, much more than we enjoy the work we do now.

Reclaiming the power to define

When I think of what humanity might look like, taking back the power to define is more important than ever. How we look at healthcare, living, success, responsibility, and dependence are a few of the key terms that need to be defined from a humanistic perspective. These new definitions must spring from new intentions based on new values and the careful shift to a new approach.

Reviewing some of what has been previously mentioned, "health care" would begin with how we design systems that meet the needs and comforts for as many as we can, if not all. It is counterproductive that healthcare be driven by profits and only treating disease. "Health care" begins with promoting a healthy lifestyle beyond diet and exercise. A healthy lifestyle includes a sense of security, the feeling of hope, the support of others, and seeing the environment around us as inviting and beautiful. All of this can be done.

"Success" will be measured by the journey as well as the results. The ends would no longer justify the means if the means are destructive in nature and not building stronger bonds and a better quality of life. "Dependence" will be a welcome part of our approach. It is not a sign of weakness. It is a demonstration that we are worthy of giving and receiving both love and support.

"Responsibility" must also be redefined. I have had many discussions about how we are having our freedoms taken from us. Yet, the freedom I have often pushed back against is the freedom to be irresponsible. Several people tell me that we should be able to eat whatever we want even if it is processed, full of chemicals, and leads to an unhealthy lifestyle. That sounds fine in a disconnected individualistic world. But the reality is there should be a level of responsibility and accountability for those who govern and those who manufacture and provide the products we eat and use.

The rest of us can then feel confident that those people in position of power are looking out for our quality of life. If we have to police the integrity of those who we elect to govern, then what is the benefit of having a governing body? If we have to monitor the responsibilities of producers of our products, then what is the responsibility of the producers? At the very least, we need to be able to easily access the true information about the products we have to choose from as consumers.

There is plenty of freedom of choice that comes with a responsible lifestyle. The fact is that we are connected and, though it may seem like you are only harming yourself when you do whatever you want, our choices do affect others. Whether the result is not being reliable, or needing other folks to clean up our mess, our decisions impact each other. The idea that we are free to do whatever we want without being accountable to the world we live in increases the chances that our decisions will cause harm. With a system designed to promote humanity, responsibility can give us the same feeling of satisfaction we seek in wanting our "freedom."

As we learn to be led by a new mind, our approach naturally differs. When we approach from a sense that we are all connected to the earth, each other, and all forms of life, we will know that the earth provides us with an abundance of what we need to live comfortable, enjoyable lives. In humanity, I have observed that we can see each other as worthy of sharing, supporting and serving rather than as competitors vying for control of our resources. We must learn the value of conflict resolution and see our differences, not as a threat, but as a demonstration of contrasting views with the same goals in mind. A curiosity in the process of redefining our values becomes a part of the approach, as does prevention of harm.

Curiosity keeps us connected

I did not learn much about other cultures from growing up in American culture. I recall my World History teacher at the Jesuit Institute telling me that Eastern Asian and African cultures did not change over time and therefore did not bring value. I immediately recognized the bogus fallacy of this belief and it hurt me to hear this. Thankfully, instead of making me bitter toward this practice of intentional ignorance, the teacher's comment inspired me to venture out. I am now able to interact with people from other cultures on an intimate level, observe the similarities and appreciate differences that I was not previously aware of.

It is important that we all stay curious and approach other humans with respect and a desire to remain connected. As long as we look to build bonds and remain open to differences, we can gain appreciation and experience new perspectives, insights, values, and more. This type of curiosity for the life of our planet and the lives around us adds to our quality of life. If quality of life becomes our priority, who knows what we can accomplish together?

A shift to prevention

We too often do not value prevention in our society because we're a capitalistic society. Capitalism makes you think of money before humanity. I'm not advocating for socialism or communism here. Rather, I'm pro humanity and life. Yet in capitalism, we have created the idea that the medium of exchange should be controlled, manipulated, even withheld and valued beyond the exchange of energy. In capitalism, the capital is what we use to measure the merit of our decisions. If that's our first thought, then we begin from a disconnected approach. Valuing finance over the human leads us to make decisions that are counter-productive to humanity. It forces us to focus on the end game, rather than prevention, making real solutions to problems impossible.

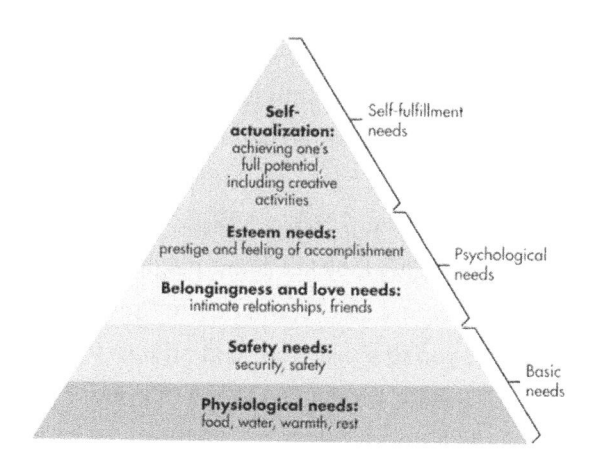

Maslow's Hierarchy of Needs pyramid:
- **Self-actualization:** achieving one's full potential, including creative activities — Self-fulfillment needs
- **Esteem needs:** prestige and feeling of accomplishment — Psychological needs
- **Belongingness and love needs:** intimate relationships, friends
- **Safety needs:** security, safety — Basic needs
- **Physiological needs:** food, water, warmth, rest

Day in and out, we make more money from the process of destroying, punishing and attempting to deal with the aftermath of the problems that our system creates, and less money from recognizing the causes and preventing negative outcomes. Let's reverse this reality and see what happens.

Take a look at Maslow's Hierarchy of Needs and how our performance is related to valuing humans first. Maslow teaches us that if your basic needs aren't met, then your ability to focus on how you show up to others is not a priority. The reason for most petty crimes and even domestic violence stems from the stress of these needs not being met. Yet we live in a world of abundance to cover all of these needs. In a world built around making sure that no child is left behind because we act as a village, then the third level of needs are taken care of by the effort to meet the first two levels of needs.

With human needs being met and supportive relationships in place, we can focus on our accomplishments and being the best version of ourselves. As such, we will be inclined to contribute to the community that supports us. With the consistent practices of these behaviors, we will become a multicultural world that promotes individual and community-based actualization and success and a level of connections that, for most of us, we can only imagine at this time.

With all this happening, there is little room for a punitive system. What does society look like if our neighbors are part of the corrections system, where they come out and see us having a bad day and say, "Hey, you look like you're in an upset mood, is there anything I can do to help? Would you like to talk about it before you go?" In a connected world, this is a common way of interacting. Imagine how much can be prevented by taking the time to care for one another.

If we took all the money that is spent on reacting to the effects that our scarcity based thinking has caused and invested it in making sure our basic needs are met, creating programs that strengthen our connection by, among other things, teaching people responsibility and accountability, self-help and development, better communication skills, etc., imagine what kind of society we could become.

So many more, if not all, of us would be able to reach their full potential and contribute meaningfully, productively, and financially. A significant initial investment would take time to actualize but would create more economic growth in the long run, in addition to allowing people to thrive. All we need is a reallocation of how we invest our energy in our society. This would be a true manifestation of humanity.

Thank You for Reading

For years, I have wanted to write a book to share what I've gained from my experiences. I had a variety of ideas of what to write about given the vast areas of our systemic racism and the multiple layers of harm we have inflicted on others and ourselves. The idea and inspiration for my method came from two places.

Part of my inspiration came when I read what President George Bush had to say about finally reckoning with the racism in our country following the murder of George Floyd. I was so enraged that he would say what he did as if he could do nothing about it, and then he did nothing about it, as if saying it was enough. It was the same feeling I felt hearing Hillary Clinton speak about the Flint Michigan water crisis and then do nothing about it. Still to this day, there are water crises in Flint and Detroit Michigan. Of course, they are in the areas mostly populated by melanated humans.

As different as the two political parties seems to be in our white world, one area of similarity is that repairing the harm of racism remains mainly in the discussion phase at best. I wrote an 8-page response to how to solve racism as Bush suggested in his speech. I let Vinnie, a close friend and someone I value as a writer, read what I wrote. He said, "It's great, you really should expand all these points in your book." As I let several others who are involved in white anti-racism groups read it, they all echoed Vinnie's desire to see my arguments expanded.

The second inspiration came from an affirmation to share my story. A few young parents in the antiracism spaces told me that talking with me and hearing my story gave them hope that they too could raise children to have similar appreciation and wisdom from their experiences. They appreciated the example that my parents purposely made sure that my sisters and I were raised to socialize in a black community and not just have black friends come to our space.

I never desired to share my story in this way, but I thought about the joy I felt watching my parents interact with my friends' family in their homes. I still feel a sense of appreciation when I reflect on those moments. I was able to have living examples of what it is like to value and respect others rather than judging them based on their socio-economic status or the color of their skin. I thank my parents for allowing my sisters and I to pave our own way given that many of the experiences we had were new to all of us.

I hope that, if I have accomplished anything by writing this book, it will have been to help us realize that we can end the scourge of racism. We whites can heal from the triggers within that cause us to maintain the confusion and harm of our culture. We can value other individuals and cultures and be the best version of ourselves. We can appreciate the differences and greatness in all individuals and cultures and ourselves. We can comfortably give credit to others who have made contributions from which we have benefitted without feeling diminished. We can exchange energy in a way that connects us to each other and the earth.

I appreciate you for spending your time reading my thoughts and lessons. I only hope that this book has been received with the hopeful spirit and purpose from which I intended when I wrote it. We are on a journey together, so let's enjoy it as we face our fears, make mistakes, make corrections, and repair and heal our harm. Humanity is achievable.

In Loving Memory

Fannie "Ma" Boyd

You are the rock that all my love for black culture is built on. You welcomed me into your home and into your family and the sound of your voice still echoes in my mind. Everything I do is dedicated to you.

Lucille Sykes and Francis Duncan

You showed me love and support every day. You looked out for me and made me feel valued. I could come to talk to you about anything. You are with me every step of the way

Coach Sylvester Stevenson

You had something in you that made me excited to see you every chance I got. I was inspired for you to witness me being the best version of myself. I pray that you are proud of me.

Alderman Sam Moore

You are truly my OG. I witnessed through you what community leadership is all about. Big Mella, I will always be your Lil Mella.

Amikham

Thank you for introducing me to the Kingdom. You taught me about community building. You looked out for me and my sister as we became a part of the building of a new world.

Ben Ammi

You opened my eyes to the reality that we can create a world of peace. Your vision is still a work in progress. Your blueprint for the Kingdom of Yah is achievable. Todah Robah Ben Ammi Ha Masheakh!

Andrew Brown

You are a class act. You were my friend and mentor. You showed me support and encouraged me every step of the way. You are a true example of what being a father and husband is all about.

To my beloved grandparents

I was always welcome, even when we disagreed. You told me what you thought was best and allowed me to create my own vision. You encouraged me and you supported me throughout my journey.

Acknowledging Those Who Have Been a Major Part of My Life

Joan Mass
Larry Mass and Sue Wirthlin-Mass
The Osher Family - Khaya, Shemohn, Dor, Ami, and Shalom
Paula Mass
Rose and Robert Mass
Peter and Ann Husch
Fannie and Maurice Boyd
The Jordan Family
72uece
Chevela and Stephen Quinn
Sydnee Burgess-Logan
Nidhi Prakash
Aunts Peggy Hellman and Louise Goldberg and all the Hellman and Goldberg family.
Aunts Peg and Sally and all the Rothschild and Dean Family
Uncles Ed, Gary and Bill and all of the Mass Family
U City Alum, Teachers and Staff - Class of 92 and 93 –FOTI
Jackson Park Alum, Teachers and Staff
Brittany Woods Alum, Teachers and Staff
Chris "Topher" Jones
Rob Green
Gauntlett McCarter
Sal and Vinnie and the Tannous Family
OG Yella Ice – Keith Duncan
Sylvester Stevenson, Quinn and Julian,
Sam and Lynn Moore
Carl Walker, Cameron Thomas, and Mike Jones
Big Cornell
Rhonda Mack
The Brown family, Andrew, Jamie, Lauren and Kristen
Doug Morgan
Tony Carter
Earl Jefferson
Victor Pichon and family

The Clark Family – Josef, Shameem, Trina, Joseph and Richelle
Michelle DiStaso
Malena Amusa
PGU 2016 OMC Cohort – The Doctors Office
PGU Staff and Professors
Kingdom of Yah – Ben Ammi, Nasik Asiel, Amikham, Sar Amiel and all the saints
--- Current Support team
Hosea
Kevin Bryant
Park Place Housing & Economic Development Darrick Young and Family
Demetrius Denham and the Denham family
Vince Clardy
Tre Goodrum
Big Tone
DJ Sirrlos
KyJuan and Murphy Lee
The Team Lunatic Fam
Ernest, Debbie and the Carey's
Melinda Sue Norin
Garrett Broad
Bobby Holland
Gerald Ivory
Audrey Georg
Michele Dumont
Dahlia
Adam Smith
Matt Harper
Paul Shirey
Liz Sutton
Jason David
Shelly Tuchluck
WP4BL
AROC
My Witnessing Whiteness Cohort
Unraveling Whiteness – Kara Bender and Laura Horwitz
Rocco Chappie
GQ
Tommy Davidson
Central Reform Congregation Rabbis – Susan, Jim, Randy, Daniel and Karen
Desiree Duffy and Black Chateau
Anyone I forgot, I did not mean it. I love you

Special Thanks to Contributors Bob Gordh and Trudy Goodwin, Nicole Young, Courtney Davis, Glynis Owens, Odie McCottrell, and Elizabeth Fischer

Bibliography

Ammi, B. (1982). God the Black Man and Truth. Communicators Press Inc. Retrieved from: https://africanhebrewisraelitesofjerusalem.com/our-leadership/ben-ammi/

Askvik, E.O., F. R. (Ruud) van der Weel and Audrey L. H. van der Meer. (2020). The Importance of Cursive Handwriting Over Typewriting for Learning in the Classroom: A High-Density EEG Study of 12-Year-Old Children and Young Adults. Frontiers in Psychology https://doi.org/10.3389/fpsyg.2020.01810

Berkovec, J.A., Canner, G.B., Gabriel, S.A. and Hannan, T.H. (1996). A Journal of Policy Development and Research. Volume 2, Number 1. U.S. Department of Housing and Urban Development. Office of Policy Development and Research

Clark, K. (1963). Conversations with James Baldwin. In F. L. Standley & L. H. Pratt (Eds.), (pp. 45). Jackson, MS: University Press of Mississippi

Elliott, J. (2020). Anti-Racism activist Jane Elliott asks a simple question about Race. Retrieved from: https://www.youtube.com/watch?v=sSZpYGRd6SY

Gray, J. (2020). All the Smoke Episode 61, Showtime Basketball. Retrieved from: https://www.youtube.com/watch?v=VCve6J2Xua0&t=4782s

Humes, E. (2006). How the GI Bill Shunted Blacks into Vocational Training. Pp.92-104, No. 53. The Journal of Blacks in Higher

Education. The JBHE Foundation Inc. https://www.jstor.org/stable/i25073517

Jones, K., and Okun, T. (2001). A Workbook for Social Change Groups - The Characteristics of White Supremacy Culture. www.dismantlingracism.org

Lester, J. (1968). To Be a Slave. New York. Dial Press

Ray, R. and Perry, A.M. (2020). Why we need reparations for Black Americans. www.brookings.edu/policy2020/

Ritchie, H. (2019). Half of the world's habitable land is used for agriculture. More than three-quarters of this is used for livestock production, despite meat and dairy making up a much smaller share of the world's protein and calorie supply. Our World in Data.org. Oxford Martin School, Oxford University

Rock, C. (1999). Bigger & Blacker. Retrieved from: https://scrapsfromtheloft.com/comedy/chris-rock-bigger-blacker-1999-full-transcript/

Schneider, G.S. (2022). 'A wounded healer': Ralph Northam wraps up term in office, forged by scandal into a governor of lasting consequence. Retrieved from: https://www.washingtonpost.com/dc-md-va/2022/01/09/governor-northam-blackface-scandal-legacy/

Wise, T. (2019). Pathology of Privilege: Racism, White Denial & The Cost of Inequality. Retrieved from: https://www.youtube.com/watch?v=wzzPK3OIoJI

Made in the USA
Monee, IL
23 March 2022